D0302580

The **AA** 100 Walks in

# Wales &
# The Marches

Produced by AA Publishing

© Automobile Association Developments Limited 2004

Published by AA Publishing (a trading name of Automobile Association Developments Limited, whose registered office is Millstream, Maidenhead, Windsor, SL4 5GD; registered number 1878835)

Ordnance Survey® This product includes mapping data licensed from Ordnance Survey® with the permission of the Controller of Her Majesty's Stationery Office.

© Crown copyright 2004. All rights reserved. Licence number 399221

ISBN 0 7495 4061 3
A01960

A CIP catalogue record for this book is available from the British Library.

The contents of this book are believed correct at the time of printing. Nevertheless, the publishers cannot be held responsible for any errors or omissions or for changes in the details given in this book or for the consequences of any reliance on the information it provides. We have tried to ensure accuracy, but things do change and we would be grateful if readers would advise us of any inaccuracies they encounter. This does not affect your statutory rights.

Please write to:
AA Publishing, FH16, Fanum House, Basing View, Basingstoke RG21 4EA

Visit AA Publishing at **www.theAA.com**

Colour reproduction by:
Keene Group, Andover
Printed and bound by:
Leo Paper, China

### Acknowledgements

Researched and written by John Gillham, Tom Hutton, Nicholas Reynolds and Julie Royle

### Picture credits

All images are held in the Automobile Association's own photo library (AA World Travel Library) and were taken by the following photographers:
Front cover D Croucher; 3 A Hopkins;
5 V Bates; 6/7 I Burgum; 8 I Burgum;
9c D Croucher; 9r AA; 10 Kenya Doran.

*Opposite: Looking down on Llyn Idwal in Snowdonia*

# Contents

*Page 6: The Afon Glaslyn cuts its way through the scenic Aberglaslyn Gorge near Beddgelert*

# Wales &
# The Marches

Modern Wales has a buzz, a street credibility born of a new confidence, expressed through art, music and language. But it is still a land of dragons, of druidic landscapes, of mythical warriors, and of poetry.

# Wales & The Marches

The landscape of Wales can compete with the best of anywhere in Britain. There are high jagged mountains in the north and quiet valleys. In the south the Pembrokeshire coastline juts into a foaming sea and the Brecon Beacons soar above wooded vales. To the east are the Marches, a once-troubled land where powerful English overlords once tried to subdue an unwilling populace.

The Industrial Revolution did much to shape the landscape. The southern valleys became a byword for coal mining and iron production. In the north, whole mountainsides kept England in slate roofs. Now these workings have gone and ash and rowan are returning to the valleys, the rare chough is back and the red kite can be seen above the mountain cwms.

*Strumble Head in Pembrokeshire*

## The Black Mountains and the Brecon Beacons

In the east the Black Mountains push up against the English border. Ridges of mountain divide steep valleys – Y Grib offers airy ridge walking, with far-reaching views, west to the Beacons, and east over England. A few outliers around here also make for splendid hill walks. The Blorenge overlooks the World Heritage Site of Blaenavon; the Sugar Loaf commands fine views and its distinctive dome dominates the Abergavenny skyline.

Next are the Brecon Beacons, the high, whalebacked sweeps of sandstone that gave their name to the national park in which they stand. The loftiest, Pen y Fan, is the highest mountain in southern Britain, and also one of the most accessible.

## Pembrokeshire Coast

But South Wales also offers the finest coastal walking in Britain, in the Pembrokeshire Coast National Park, which protects a ring of dramatic clifftops from Cardigan to Tenby. Here you can follow the Pembrokeshire Coast Path National Trail for much of the way. At Strumble Head, St David's Head and nearby St Non's Bay you will see majestic rock scenery and plunging cliffs, as well as remote coves and golden sandy beaches.

Both the Marloes Peninsula and the Angle Peninsula in the mouth of Milford Haven are a treat to explore on foot. Highlights include Stackpole, Manorbier and the Gower Peninsula with its sweeping sands at Rhossili

and Oxwich Bay. Further east is Dunraven Bay, a strip of magnificent Heritage Coast in south Glamorgan.

## Moorlands and Valleys

Approaching from the east, the airy moorlands rise up from the English plain. Montgomery and Welshpool make good bases to explore the borderlands. The next valley over carries the River Dee, and walks around Llangollen and Valle Crucis. Further west you will be rewarded with a fine stroll around Bala and Llyn Tegid. Perhaps the best-known uplands in this eastern march are the Berwyns, with one of Wales's loveliest waterfalls, Pistyll Rhaeadr.

## Clwydian Range

The Clwydian Range is also a highlight in the east, and the ascent of Moel Famau from Loggerheads is another classic walk. The short stroll into the Prestatyn Hillside Nature Reserve is where Offa's Dyke, the 182-mile (293km) National Trail begins. At

'Greenfield near Holywell you'll discover Basingwerk Abbey in a valley which is now a heritage park.

## Snowdonia

Inevitably you will be drawn along the coast, to Conwy and a lovely stroll on

the 'Mountain' above the town. Follow that ridge of hills along and you will encounter some real mountains, the ancient settlement sites and stone circles on Tal y Fan, then beneath the towering massif of the Carneddau at the Bwlch y Ddeufaen, a high

*Above: Offa's Dyke in South Wales*
*Left: Spectacular Pistyll Rhaedr waterfall in the Berwyns*

mountain pass above the valley of Nant-y-Coed. There are few mountain scenes in Britain that surpass Llyn Idwal, beneath the cliffs of the Twll Du, better known as the Devil's Kitchen. The Llugwy Valley, too, shows the towering heights of Snowdon to their greatest effect, viewed from Capel Curig across the twin lakes of Llynnau Mymbyr. You might want to find an easy way up Snowdon, or avoid the crowds and pick of shapely Cnicht. Snowdonia is not all summits: there is a wooded walk around Llyn Crafnant and Llyn Geirionydd.

**Anglesey**

Ynys Mon, or Anglesey, has a secret mountain on its west coast. At Holyhead you can climb high above the Irish Sea. On the opposite side of the island, Moelfre has its own history of shipwrecks and rescues.

**Mid Wales**

The Mawddach spills out to the sea at Barmouth, its estuary framed by

woodlands and crags. You're in a very seldom-visited tract of mid Wales, and yet visible to the hordes in the Brecon Beacons and Snowdonia.

to find Castell y Bere, a great fortress in the Dysynni Valley and Pumlumon, the lonely peak standing above a

**The Borderlands**

The River Wye meanders through green pastureland as it makes its way south from the cathedral city of Hereford to the Forest of Dean through prime agricultural land. The mighty River Severn is the silver thread which binds together these lush fields, bordered by the whaleback spine of the Malvern Hills to the west and Bredon Hill and the Cotswolds to the east. Here you'll find the cathedral of Worcester and the villages where half-timbered houses still survive. Shropshire's hills are dominated by the north-east/ south-west ridges of the Stiperstones, the Long Mynd and Wenlock Edge to the east. It is a surprisingly wild part of the Midlands, where heather-covered hills rise from steep-sided valleys.

*Broadway Tower in Worcestershire*

# Using this Book

**❶ Information panels**
Information panels show the total distance and total amount of ascent (that is how much ascent you will accumulate throughout the walk). An indication of the gradient you will encounter is shown by the rating 0–3. Zero indicates fairly flat ground and 3 indicates undulating terrain with several very steep slopes.

**❷ Minimum time**
The minimum time suggested is for approximate guidance only. It assumes reasonably fit walkers and doesn't allow for stops.

**❸ Start points**
The start of each walk is given as a six-figure grid reference prefixed by two letters indicating which 100km square of the National Grid it refers to. You'll find more information about grid references on most Ordnance Survey maps.

## Map legend

| | | | | |
|---|---|---|---|---|
| →→ | Walk route | | P | Car park |
| ···· | Optional walk route | | | Cliff |
| ···· | Adjoining footpath | | | Rock outcrop |
| – – – | County boundary | | | Beach |
| ☼ | Viewpoint | | | Woodland |
| ▲ 392 | Spot height | | | Parkland |
| | Built-up area | | ✝ | Church, cathedral, chapel |
| ● | Place of interest | | WC | Toilet |
| △ | Steep section | | ⚲ | Picnic area |

---

| 00 | **Location** Walk title |
|---|---|

**County** • Region

½ 2 miles (7.2km)  1hr 45min  **Ascent:** 131ft (40m) ▲

**Paths:** Cliff top, shingle beach, farm track and country lanes, 1 stile

**Suggested map:** OS Explorer 231 Southwold & Bungay

**Grid reference:** TM 522818

**Parking:** On street near Covehithe church

**See the effects of coastal erosion on a walk along a rapidly disappearing cliff top.**

**1** Take tarmac lane from **St Andrew's Church** down towards sea to barrier ('Danger') and sign warning that there is no public right of way. Although this is strictly true, this is well-established and popular path stretching north towards Kessingland beach and you are likely to meet many other walkers. The warnings are serious but it is quite safe to walk here so long as you keep away from the cliff edge.

**2** Walk through gap to **R** of road barrier and continue towards cliffs. Turn **L** along wide farm track with pig farm to your L. Path follows cliff top then descends towards beach to enter **Benacre** nature reserve. On L. is **Benacre Broad**, once an estuary, now a marshy lagoon. The shingle beach attracts little terns in spring and summer and you should keep to the path to avoid their nesting sites.

**3** Climb back on to cliffs at end of Benacre Broad. The way cuts through pine trees and bracken on constantly changing path before running alongside field and swinging **R** to descend to beach level, where you take wide grass track on your L across dunes.

**4** At concrete track, with tower of Kessingland church in distance, turn **L** following waymarks of **Suffolk Coast and Heaths Path**. Cross stile and keep straight ahead, passing **Beach Farm** on R. Stay straight ahead for 1 mile (1.6km) on wide track between fields with views of Benacre church ahead.

**5** Go through white gates and turn **L** on to quiet country lane. Stay on lane for ¾ mile (1.2km) as it passes between hedges with arable farmland to either side and swings **L** at entrance to **Half Farm**.

**6** When road bends R, turn **L** past gate with an English Nature 'No Entry' sign for cars. Stay on this permissive path as it swings **R** around meadow and continues into woodland of **Holly Grove**. Pass through another gate and turn **L** along road for ¾ mile (1.2km) back into **Covehithe**. Turn **L** at junction to return to **St Andrew's Church**.

---

## 4 Abbreviations

Walk directions use these abbreviations:

**L** – left
**L-H** – left-hand
**R** – right
**R-H** – right-hand

Names which appear on signposts are given in brackets, for example ('Bantam Beach').

## 5 Suggested maps

Details of appropriate maps are given for each walk, and usually refer to 1:25,000 scale Ordnance Survey Explorer maps. We strongly recommend that you always take the appropriate OS map with you. Our hand-drawn maps are there to give you the route and do not show all the details or relief that you will need to navigate around the routes provided in this collection. You can purchase OS maps at all good bookshops, or by calling Stanfords on 020 7836 2260.

## 6 Car parking

Many of the car parks suggested are public, but occasionally you may find you have to park on the roadside or in a lay-by. Please be considerate when you leave your car, ensuring that access roads or gates are not blocked and that other vehicles can pass safely. Remember that pub car parks are private and should not be used unless you are visiting the pub or you have the landlord's permission to park there.

# Dunraven Along the Heritage Coast

**6 miles (9.7km)** 2hrs 30min **Ascent:** 460ft (140m) ▲

**Paths:** Easy-to-follow paths across farmland and coastline, 5 stiles

**Suggested map:** OS Explorer 151 Cardiff & Bridgend

**Grid reference:** SS 885731

**Parking:** Large car park at Heritage Centre above Dunraven Beach

**Note:** Dogs are not allowed on Dunraven Beach in summer

**A pleasant foray through rolling sand dunes.**

**❶** Head up lane at back of car park and pass **Heritage Centre** on R. Keep ahead on narrow path that ducks into woodland; continue to stile. Cross it and walk along field edge to gate on L. Go through then cross stile on **R** to continue with hedge to your R.

**❷** Cross into field and keep to **L-H** side, following hedgerow, now L. At next stile, keep ahead, go past gate on L, to reach stile on **L**. Cross it and head diagonally **R** to stile between house and farmyard.

**❸** Turn **L** on to road and walk into village. Keep **L** into Southerndown Road then fork **R** into Heol-y-slough. Follow road for ¾ mile (1.2km) then, as road bends to L, keep straight across common. Continue ahead where bridleway crosses track. As you join another track, maintain direction along valley floor.

**❹** Path winds down through sand dunes, passing tributary valley on L, and eventually emerges on

B4524. Cross road and continue until you locate one of many paths that lead **L** towards **Portobello House.** At drive, keep **R** then fork **L** by house to continue through bracken, parallel to estuary of **Ogmore River.**

**❺** Stay above small cliffs near mouth of estuary and eventually arrive at parking area above beach. From here, follow obvious route along coast around to **L.**

**❻** You reach dry-stone wall, which funnels you through marked gate ('Coast Path – Emergency Vehicles Only'). Continue along coast path until, about 1¼ miles (2km) from gate, you meet with steep valley. Turn **L** into valley then immediately **R**, on to footpath that climbs steeply up grassy hillside.

**❼** Stay with footpath as it follows line of dry-stone wall around to **West Farm**. Keep to **R-H** side of agricultural buildings and continue to reach upper car park. Gap in wall, at back of this, leads you to grassy track that follows road down into **Dunraven.**

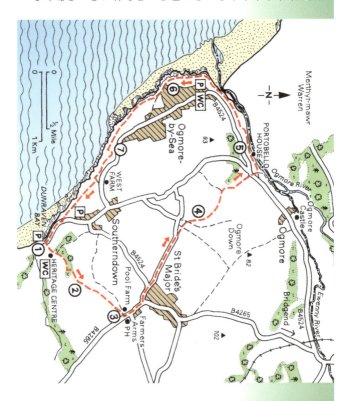

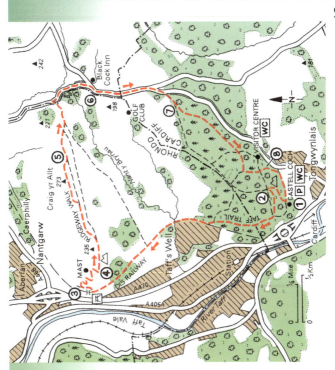

# Castell Coch Fairy-tale Castle

**5½ miles (8.8km)** 2hrs 30min **Ascent:** 920ft (280m) ▲

**Paths:** Forest tracks, disused railway line and clear paths, short section of tarmac, 2 stiles

**Suggested map:** OS Explorer 151 Cardiff & Bridgend

**Grid reference:** ST 131826

**Parking:** Castell Coch

### From a fairy-tale castle to a wild hillside.

**1** From car park, walk up to castle entrance and keep **R** to find information plaque and waymarker indicating woodland walk. Take this path and drop slightly before climbing steeply up to junction of tracks.

**2** Turn sharp **L** ('The Taff Trail') by picture of viaduct. Follow broad forest track around hillside then down, where it meets disused railway line. Continue along this for over 1 mile (1.6km) until you pass picnic area and come to barrier.

**3** Go through barrier then, as you come to disused bridge, turn **R** over stile ('Ridgeway Walk'). Take this up to junction by gate on L; turn **R**. Turn sharp **L** to zig-zag back across hillside, where you turn **R** again. Follow this around to **L** again, aiming at **mast** then, as you reach field edge, bear **R** again. This leads up to narrow ridge; turn **L**.

**4** Climb steeply up ridge and continue, with high

ground to L, to waymarker that directs you up narrow track to ridge top. Bear **R** and keep ahead until it starts to drop. Keep **R** to drop to another track; bear **L**.

**5** Follow it down through bracken to open area with stile. Cross and take track down to gate that leads on to tarmac drive. Turn **L**. Continue past houses on R-H side to junction. Turn **R** and climb up to another junction; bear **R**.

**6** Continue past **golf club**, then fork **R** on to narrow lane that drops and bears around to L. Turn **R** here to walk past Forestry Commission sign then **L**, on to narrow footpath marked by yellow-ringed post.

**7** Follow this path, ignoring tracks on both R and L, until posts become blue and you reach T-junction by sign forbidding horse riding. Turn **L** here, where posts are once again yellow, and continue downhill, past turning on L to **Countryside Visitor Centre.**

**8** Track swings around to **R** and descends to meet drive. Turn **R** to climb up drive and back to **castle.**

# Rhossili The Highs and Lows

**4 miles (6.4km)** 1hr 45min **Ascent:** 590ft (180m) ⚠

**Paths:** Easy-to-follow footpaths across grassy downs, 2 stiles

**Suggested map:** OS Explorer 164 Gower

**Grid reference:** SS 416880

**Parking:** Large car park at end of road in Rhossili

**This walk takes in the stunning views over one of Wales's finest and wildest beaches.**

❶ From car park, head out on to road and continue uphill as if you were walking back out of village. You'll pass **St Mary's Church** on your L then, immediately after this, bear **L** down on broad track to gate. Go through gate and keep **L** to follow grassy track that snakes along steep hillside.

❷ Follow this through bracken, passing **Old Rectory** on your L, and eventually you'll reach sunken section with wall on your L, and **caravan park** behind. Don't be tempted to break off R just yet; instead, keep going until you come to gate. You might spot the crumbled timber skeleton of the *Helvetica* protruding from the sands below at low tide. More than one ship has fallen foul of the cruel storms that pound Rhossili. The *Helvetica* was washed up here in November 1887, but miraculously her five-man crew all survived.

❸ Turn sharp **R** here and follow grassy track steeply

up on to ridge. Of all the Gower beaches, none are blessed with quite the untamed splendour of **Rhossili Bay**. This sweeping expanse of sand runs for 4 miles (6.4km) from the Worms Head to the stranded outcrop of Burry Holms, upon which sits a ruined chapel. At top of steep section it's easy to be drawn off to R towards some obvious outcrops, but keep to top track that literally follows crest.

❹ Pass some ancient cairns and drop slightly to pass pair of megalithic cromlechs, or burial chambers. These are known as **Sweyne's Howes** and are over 4,000 years old. Continue on broad track up to high point of **The Beacon**.

❺ Keep straight ahead on clear track that starts to drop easily then steepens to meet dry-stone wall. Continue walking down side of wall and eventually come to gate you passed through on way out.

❻ Follow lane out to road, turn **R** and pass **St Mary's Church** on your R to return to car park.

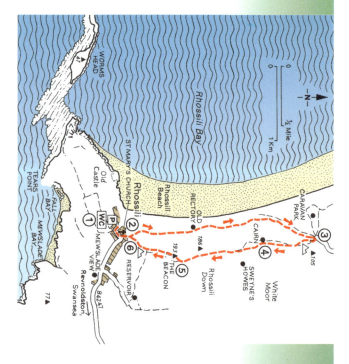

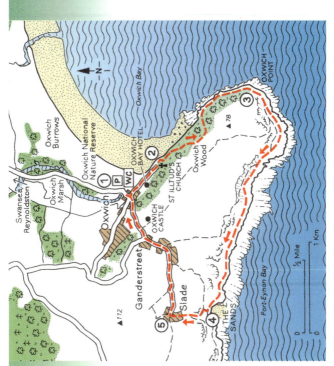

# Oxwich Woodland and Coast

**4½ miles (7.2km)** 2hrs **Ascent:** 480ft (146m) ⚠

**Paths:** Clear paths through woodland, along coast and across farmland, quiet lane, 6 stiles

**Suggested map:** OS Explorer 164 Gower

**Grid reference:** SS 500864

**Parking:** Oxwich Bay

**An exhilarating ramble through woodland and along delightful coastline.**

❶ **Oxwich** village was once a busy port that paid its way by shipping limestone from the local quarries, but it's now one of the prettiest and most unspoilt Gower villages, due in no small part to its distance from main roads. For maximum enjoyment it is best visited away from the main holiday season. Walk back out of the car park and turn **L** to crossroads. Turn **L** here (waymarked 'Eglwys') and pass Woodside Guesthouse and **Oxwich Bay Hotel**, on your **R**. This lane leads into woods and up to 6th-century **St Illtud's Church**, where gate marks end of road and start of path leading out on to **Oxwich Point**.

❷ Go through gate and bear **R**, going up some wooden steps to climb steeply up through wood. As footpath levels, bear **L** to drop back down through wood and around headland until it comes out into open above **Oxwich Point**.

❸ Path drops through gorse and bracken to become grassy coast path that runs easily above rocky beach. Keep sea on your **L** and ignore any tracks that run off to **R**. After approximately 1 mile (1.6km) you'll pass distinct valley that drops in from your **R**. Continue past this and cross succession of stiles, until you reach sandy beach of **The Sands**.

❹ Turn **R**, behind beach, and follow narrow footpath to stile. This leads on to broad farm track, where you turn **L**. Continue up and around to **R** until you come to galvanised kissing gate. Go through this and keep **R** to head up lane past some houses to crossroads.

❺ Turn **R** here and follow road along to fork where you keep **R**. Drop down to entrance of **Oxwich Castle** on **R**. This is a 16th-century mansion built by Sir Rhys Mansel on the site of a 14th-century castle, hence the name. After looking at or exploring the castle, turn **R**, back on to lane, and head down into **Oxwich** village. Keep straight ahead to car park.

**Paths:** Coast path for the whole distance, 8 stiles
**Suggested map:** OS Explorer 164 Gower
**Grid reference:** SS 467851
**Parking:** Large car park in Port-Eynon (buses provide logistical links on this linear route)

**6½ miles (10.4km) 3hrs Ascent: 850ft (260m)** ▲

**A linear trek along the most scenic stretch of the Gower Coast.**

❶ From car park head towards sea, following broad sandy track that leads past **Youth Hostel** and then on to ruins of **Salt House**, where an information board gives plenty of history on the area. Continue behind beach then fork **R** to climb steeply past quarry to **obelisk** at top.

❷ Follow cliff tops along and drop to stile. Cross this to walk behind rocky beach. Keep **R** at fork to climb slightly, then drop **L** down some steps to 2nd stile. Cross this and follow path as it squeezes between impressive limestone cliffs and steep scree. You'll hurdle rocky terrace and drop beneath more crags before heading down to reach broken wall.

❸ Cross wall and turn **R** to climb up steeply to good path. Turn **L** on to this and follow wall to **Foxhole Slade**. Cross iron stile in dip and climb steeply back up. (This area is owned by the National Trust) After

200 yards (183m), next to gate on R, fork **L**. Don't be drawn out on to coast, instead continue in same direction until you join wall again and drop to stile.

❹ Cross this and bear **L** back out on to cliff top. Cross stile and continue to fence, which you then follow to head of huge hollow. Cross behind this and continue along line of wall to **Mew Slade**. As wall bears R, keep straight ahead on steep path that drops awkwardly into valley.

❺ Turn **L** at bottom, and drop to stile on **R**. Cross this to small cove and then follow narrow path that contours around hillside to rejoin main coast path above. Bear **L** on to this and continue to another dip. Keep high to round head of valley and then drop down, with wall on your R.

❻ Leave wall to head back up grassy down to cliff tops where you veer around to **R** to follow them along. To continue to **Rhossili**, walk past car park to bus stop on **L** by **St Mary's Church**.

16

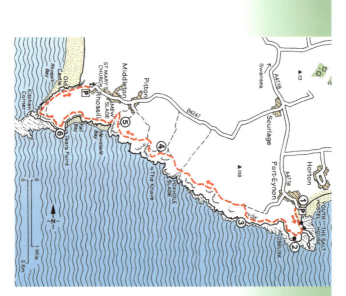

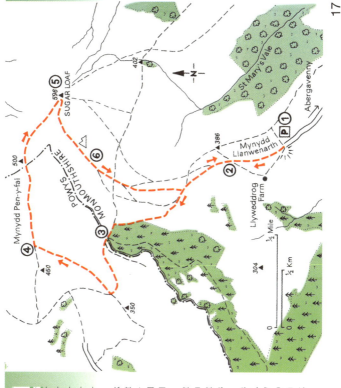

# Sugar Loaf Sweet Walking

**4½ miles (7.2km)** 2hrs 30min **Ascent:** 1,150ft (350m) ⚑

Paths: Grassy tracks, no stiles

**Suggested map:** OS Explorer 0L13 Brecon Beacons National Park Eastern area

**Grid reference:** SO 268167

**Parking:** Top of small lane running north from A40, to west of Abergavenny

**Escape the crowds and see another side of one of the most distinctive and popular of the Abergavenny peaks.**

❶ Standing in car park and looking up slope you'll see 3 obvious tracks leading away. The lowest, down to L, is tarmac drive; above this, but still heading out L, is broad grassy track. Take this and follow it for 500yds (457m) to corner of dry-stone wall.

❷ This marks crossroads where you keep straight ahead, to follow wall on your L. Continue along this line for another ½ mile (800m), ignoring any R forks, and keeping wall down to your L. Eventually, you'll start to drop down into valley, where you leave wall and head diagonally towards wood. At end of the wood, keep **L** to descend grassy path to stream.

❸ Climb out of valley, keeping to steepest, **R–H** path. This leads around shoulder and meets another dry-stone wall. Follow this, still climbing a little, until it levels by corner and gate in wall. Turn **R** here, cross

some lumpy ground and follow grassy path up.

❹ As track levels, you'll be joined by another track from L. Continue ahead and climb on to rocks at western end of summit ridge. Follow ridge to white-painted trig point on **Sugar Loaf**. The **Sugar Loaf** and some of the land around it belongs to the National Trust, who own about 4% of the National Parks.

❺ Looking back towards car park, you'll see that hillside is criss-crossed with tracks. Most will lead you back eventually, but easiest route follows path that traverses **R**, from directly below trig point. This veers **L** and drops steeply down blunt spur.

❻ Follow this past insignificant R fork and then as path levels, carry straight ahead at crossroads. Keep **L** at another fork, then bear **R** at next to follow almost sunken track along broken wall, which leads to junction by a wall. This is track that you followed on your outward leg. Bear **L** and retrace your steps back to car park.

# Blorenge Bird's-eye View of Abergavenny

**3 miles (4.8km)** 1hr 30min **Ascent:** 530ft (161m) ▲

**Paths:** Clear tracks over open mountainside, quiet lane, no stiles

**Suggested map:** OS Explorer OL13 Brecon Beacons National Park Eastern area

**Grid reference:** SO 270109

**Parking:** Small car park at Carn-y-gorfydd

**A short sortie and some marvellous views.**

**1** There's no easier peak to climb in the Brecon Beacons National Park but there are also few that occupy such a commanding position. The English sounding name – Blorenge – probably derives from 'blue ridge' and the mountain actually dominates a small finger of the National Park that points southwards from Abergavenny to Pontypool. It also marks a watershed between the protected mountain scenery that makes up the bulk of the National Park and the ravaged landscape that forms the southern boundary. Along the way look out and listen for red grouse as this is one of the best places in South Wales to see them as they were once managed on these moors. You'll usually be alerted to their presence by a frantic stabbing, alarmed clucking followed by a frantic escape flight. From **Carn-y-gorfydd** Roadside Rest, walk downhill for 500yds (457m) and bear **L**, through green barrier, on to grassy track.

**2** This leads easily uphill, through a tangle of bracken, eventually allowing great views over the Usk Valley towards the outlying peak of Ysgyryd Fawr.

**3** As path levels you'll pass small **hut**. Continue along escarpment edge, on one of series of terraces that contour above steep escarpment, and enjoy the views over Abergavenny and the Black Mountains. The rough ground was formed by the quarrying of stone.

**4** Return to **hut** and bear **R**, on to clear, grassy track that climbs slightly and becomes stony. Away to R, you should be able to make out pronounced hump of Bronze-Age burial cairn. The path now leads easily to **trig point** and huge **cairn** that marks summit.

**5** Maintain same direction, drop down past limestone outcrop and towards **masts** on skyline. You should also be able to see the extensive spoil heaps on the flanks of Gilwern Hill, directly ahead.

**6** At masts, you'll meet road; turn **L** and continue easily downhill, for 600yds (549m), back to start.

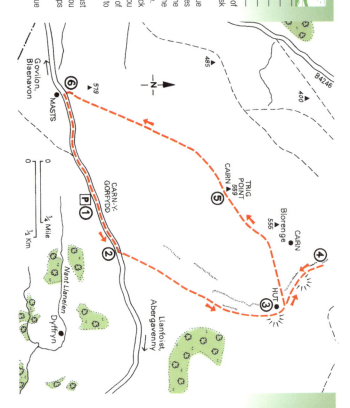

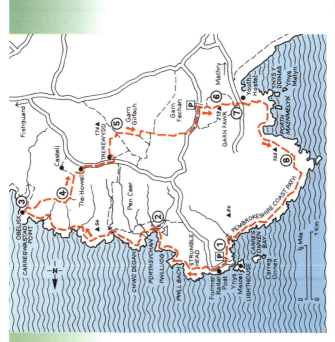

# Strumble Head An Invigorating Trundle

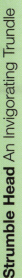

**8 miles (12.9km)** 3hrs 30min **Ascent:** 920ft (280m) ▲

**Paths:** Coast path, grassy, sometimes muddy tracks, rocky paths, 21 stiles

**Suggested map:** OS Explorer OL35 North Pembrokeshire

**Grid reference:** SM 894411

**Parking:** Car park by Strumble Head Lighthouse

**A walk in the coast's wildest countryside.**

**1** Walk back up road and cross stile on **L** on to coast path. Pass above bays of **Pwll Bach** and **Pwllug**; drop steeply to footbridge behind pebble beach of **Porthsychan**.

**2** Follow coast path waymarkers around **Cnwc Degan** and down to bridge, where 2 footpaths lead away from coast. Continue along coast, past cottage on **R** then climbing and dropping a couple of times, before you reach **obelisk** at **Carregwastad Point**.

**3** Follow track inland and cross stile on to track; turn **R**, away from coast path. Continue with path up through gorse wall; turn **R** on to good track. Take this through succession of gates and around **L-H** bend.

**4** Ignore track to **R** and continue up cattle track to farmyard where you swing **R** then **L**, after buildings, to road. Turn **R** and follow road past large house to waymarked bridleway on **L**. Pass **Trenewydd** and go through gate on to green lane. Follow this up to

another gate and on to open ground.

**5** Turn **R** here; follow wall to gate to walled track; follow it to road. Turn **L**; climb up to car park beneath **Garn Fawr**. Turn **R**, on to hedged track, and follow this up, through gap in wall, and over rocks to trig point.

**6** Climb down and cross saddle between this tor and another, slightly lower, to south. From here head west towards even lower outcrop and pass it on **L**. This becomes clear path that leads down to stile. Cross this. Turn **L**, then **R** on to drive to road.

**7** Walk straight across and then on to coast path. Bear **R**; cross stile to drop down towards **Ynys y Ddinas**, small island ahead. Navigation is easy as you continue on coast path north, over **Porth Maenmelyn** and up to cairn.

**8** Continue along coast, towards lighthouse, until you drop to footbridge above **Carreg Onnen Bay**. Cross stile into field, then another back on to coast path and return to car park.

# St David's Head A Rocky Ramble

**3½ miles (5.7km)** **2hrs** **Ascent:** 425ft (130m) ▲

**Paths:** Coast path, clear paths across heathland, 2 stiles

**Suggested map:** OS Explorer OL35 North Pembrokeshire

**Grid reference:** SM 734271

**Parking:** Whitesands Beach

**An easy stroll around dramatic cliffs.**

**①** St David's Head is steeped in legend and peppered with the evidence of ancient civilizations. It would be difficult to imagine a more atmospheric place and for its full effect visit at sunset and watch the sky turn red over the scattered islets of the Bishops and the Clerks, located on the west of the headland. From **Whitesands Beach** head back up the road, pass **campsite**, and track on **L**, and then take 2nd track on **L**. Bear **R** where it splits and continue around **L-H** bend to walk up to buildings. Keep **L** to walk between houses and then carry on to gate.

**②** Turn **R** on to open heathland and follow footpath along wall beneath **Carn Llidi**. Pass track that drops to **youth hostel** on **R** and continue around to where the path splits. Take higher track and keep going in same direction until, at corner of wall, clear track runs diagonally **L** towards coast.

**③** Follow this to coast path and turn **L** to hug cliff

tops. At **Porth Llong**, path bears **R** to climb to cairn. You'll find that the headland is a labyrinth of paths and tracks, but for maximum enjoyment try to stick as close to the cliff tops as possible as you round a number of narrow zawns. The official coast path doesn't go as far as the tip of the peninsula, but plenty of other tracks do, so follow one as far as you wish.

**④** From tip, turn **L** and make your way through rocky outcrops on southern side of headland. As you approach **Porthmelgan** you'll pick up obvious path that traverses steep hillside down into valley, which shelters small stream.

**⑤** Cross stream and climb up steps on other side. Continue to kissing gate where National Trust land ends and maintain your direction. Pass above **Porth Lleuog** and distinctive rocky promontory of **Trwynhwrddyn**, which is worth a visit.

**⑥** Path then drops steeply down to road at entrance to **Whitesands Beach**.

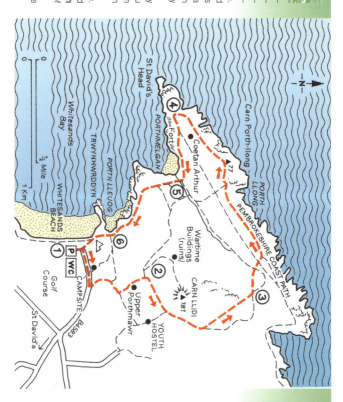

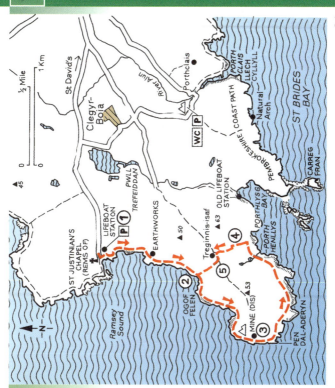

# Ramsey Sound Pounding the Hermit Monk

3½ miles (5.7km) 2hrs **Ascent:** 197ft (60m) ⛰

**Paths:** Coast path and easy farmland tracks, 5 stiles
**Suggested map:** OS Explorer 0L35 North Pembrokeshire
**Grid reference:** SM 724252
**Parking:** Car park above lifeboat station at St Justinian's

**Along the shores of Ramsey Sound with great views and plenty of opportunities for spotting wildlife.**

**1** This is an easy but very rewarding walk with gorgeous coastal scenery and it is worth keeping a pair of binoculars handy as there are plenty of chances to spot seals, porpoises, dolphins, choughs and even Peregrine falcons along the way. Walk down to **lifeboat station** and then turn **L** on to coast path, above steps. Follow this, passing above a number of lofty, grassy promontories that make great picnic spots. After ½ mile (800m), look out for traces of Iron-Age **earthworks** on your **L**.

**2** Pass gate and track on your **L** – this is your return route – and swing around to west above **Ogof Felen**. This is a good seal pup beach in autumn. Trail climbs slightly and then drops steeply to ruined copper mine, directly opposite The Bitches.

**3** Continue easily to **Pen Dal-aderyn** and then swing eastwards to enter **St Brides Bay**. Path climbs above some magnificent cliffs and passes between a few rocky outcrops before veering north above broad bay of **Porth Henllys**. Drop down into shallow valley until you come to fingerpost at junction of paths.

**4** Turn **L** and cross stile on **R**, into field. Turn **L** to follow track along wall to another gate, where you enter courtyard. Keep **L** here and pass barn on **L**. When track opens out into field, keep **R** to pass through gate and on to waymarked track.

**5** Follow this waymarked track down between dry-stone walls to reach another gate, which leads back out on to coast path. Turn **R** and retrace your outward route along grassy clifftop path back to **St Justinian's**. While you're here it is worth taking a boat trip to Ramsey Island. As well as getting a close-up look at the seal colonies on the western flanks, you'll also get views of the rushing waters of The Bitches but you'll need waterproofs as it can get pretty wet.

3½ **miles (5.7km)** 1hr 30min **Ascent:** 262ft (80m) ▲

**Paths:** Coast path and clear footpaths over farmland, 6 stiles

**Suggested map:** OS Explorer OL35 North Pembrokeshire

**Grid reference:** SM 757252

**Parking:** Pay-and-display car park in St David's

**Easy walking around the coastline that gave birth to the Welsh patron saint, St David.**

❶ Turn **L** out of car park in **St David's** and walk down road, as if you were heading for **Caerfai Bay**. As houses thin out, you'll see turning on **R** that leads to more dwellings. Take this and then turn **L** on to waymarked bridleway. Follow this bridleway between hedges, past end of road and go on to junction with another road.

❷ Walk straight across and then take waymarked path down pleasant track to stile. Cross over and keep to **L** of field to another stile, where you keep straight ahead again. This leads to farmyard, which is also caravan park.

❸ Turn **R** and keep hedge on your R, where drive swings off to L. Continue across this field and at end drop down between gorse bushes to road at **Porth Clais.** Turn **L** to bottom of valley and then, before crossing bridge, turn **L** on to coast path.

❹ Climb up steeply on to cliff tops and bear around to L to walk towards **Porth y Ffynnon.** The next small headland is **Trwyn Cynddeiriog,** where there's a lovely grassy platform above the cliffs if you fancy a rest. This is where St Non and Sant, St David's parents, were said to have lived. Continue walking into **St Non's Bay** and look for footpath on **L** that leads to ruined **chapel,** where St David is believed to have been born in the 13th century.

❺ From chapel, head up to reach gate that leads to **St Non's Well** and, from there, follow path beneath new chapel and back out on to coast path. Turn **L** to climb easily on to **Pen y Cyfrwy,** continue around this and drop down towards **Caerfai Bay.**

❻ You'll eventually come out beneath the Caerfai Bay car park where you turn **L** on to road. Follow this past the **Diving Centre** to **St David's** and start of walk. While you're in St David's Don't miss the opportunity to look around the **cathedral.**

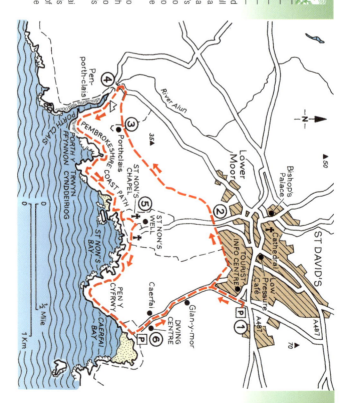

# Broad Haven The Haroldston Woods

**3½ miles (5.7km)** 1hr 30min **Ascent:** 290ft (88m)

**Paths:** Woodland trail, country lanes and coast path, 1 stile

**Suggested map:** OS Explorer OL36 South Pembrokeshire

**Grid reference:** SM 863140

**Parking:** Car park by tourist information centre in Broad Haven

**A winding path through woodland then an easy stroll above the Haroldston cliffs.**

❶ From anywhere in car park, walk towards National Park **information centre** and follow waymarked path ('Woodland Walk') that runs between information centre and coastguard rescue building. Go **R** and then **L** to bridge. Cross over bridge and continue straight ahead through kissing gate, with stream on your **L**.

❷ Ignore faint path forking to **R** and continue, on boardwalk, through wood. After ½ mile (800m) you'll come to waymarked path on **L**; ignore this and keep straight ahead until you arrive at junction of paths beneath small **chapel** on your **R**.

❸ Turn **L** to road and then **R** on to it to walk uphill, with church on your **R**. Keep ahead at T-junction, then take 1st **L** towards Druidston Haven. Follow this over cattle grid to sharp **R-H** bend. (As you turn the bend note the good track running parallel to the road in a

field to your **L**. This is an ancient trade route, known as the Welsh Way, that runs from Monk's Haven or St Ishmael's, to Whitesands Beach.) Continue for another 300yds (274m) to reach small parking area and gate on your **L**.

❹ Go through this and follow well-surfaced track down towards coast. On reaching cliff tops, bear around to **L** and continue past the crumbled remains of an Iron-Age fort on **Black Point**.

❺ After passing **Harold Stone** on your **L** (the stone is believed to mark the spot where Harold, the Earl of Wessex, defeated the Welsh in the 11th century), path starts to drop, generally quite easily but there is one steep step. Follow path down to meet road and keep **R** to drop to walkway above beach.

❻ Cross over bridge and then, just before road you are on merges into main road, turn **L** on tarmac footpath that leads through green and back to car park at start.

# Marloes Island Views

**6 miles (9.7km)** 2hrs 30min **Ascent:** 420ft (128m) ▲

**Paths:** Coast path and clear footpaths, short section on tarmac, 10 stiles

**Suggested map:** OS Explorer OL36 South Pembrokeshire

**Grid reference:** SM 761089

**Parking:** National Trust car park above Martin's Haven, near Marloes village

**Around a windswept headland overlooking two islands and a marine nature reserve.**

❶ From car park turn **L** on to road and walk down to bottom of hill. Bear around to **L** and then go through gate straight ahead into Deer Park. Turn **L** and follow path along to stile and out on to coast.

❷ With sea to your **R**, continue easily along over **Deadman's Bay** to another stile. Next section cruises along easily, passing earthworks of Iron-Age **fort** on **L** and crosses another stile as you approach **Gateholm Island.**

❸ It is possible to get across to the island at low tide, but care is needed to scramble over the slippery rocks. To continue walk, follow coast path, above western end of beautiful **Marloes Sands** until you drop easily to main beach access path. If you are walking in the spring or summer you'll be impressed by the small white and pink flowers that carpet the cliff tops. These are sea campion (white) and thrift (pink)

and both are common along the Pembrokeshire coast.

❹ Turn **L** and climb up to road; turn **R** here. Follow road along for around ¾ mile (1.2km) to bridleway on **L**. Follow this down and turn **L** into **Marloes** village.

❺ Pass **Lobster Pot** on **L** and continue ahead to leave village. Ignore few tracks on **R**, as road bends around to **L**, and continue out into open countryside where you'll meet footpath on **R**.

❻ Walk down edge of field and bear around to **L** to drop back down on to coast path above **Musselwick Sands.** Turn **L** and follow path west for over 1½ miles (2.4km) to **Martin's Haven.** The Dale Princess, a 50-seat passenger boat, departs from Martin's Haven for Skomer Island regularly every morning during the summer and returns during the afternoon. As well as the wildlife and relics of ancient civilizations, there's also some fine walking. Please note that dogs are not allowed on the island. Meet road and climb past **information centre** back to car park.

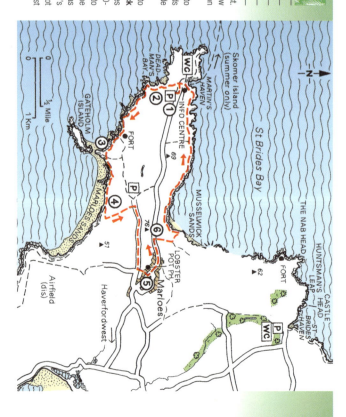

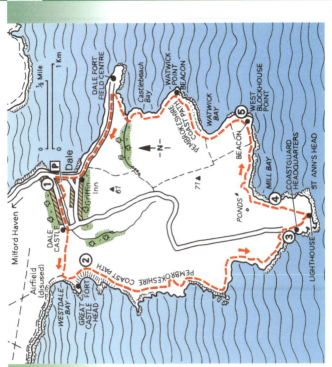

# Milford Haven A Stroll around St Ann's Head

**6½ miles (10.4km)** 3hrs **Ascent:** 590ft (180m) ⛰

**Paths:** Coast path and clear paths across farmland, 20 stiles

**Suggested map:** OS Explorer OL36 South Pembrokeshire

**Grid reference:** SM 812058

**Parking:** Large car park next to the beach in Dale

**Easy navigation and superb coastal scenery at the mouth of Milford Haven.**

❶ Leave car park by exit at the rear and follow drive to road. Turn **L** and walk to sharp **L** turn, by **Dale Castle**, where footpath leads straight ahead. Follow this up through 2 fields to stile that leads on to **Coast Path** above **Westdale Bay**. Turn **L** and climb steps up on to **Great Castle Head**, occupied by Iron-Age **fort**.

❷ For next 2 miles (3.2km), continue easily along **Coast Path** with sea to your R and farmland to your L. Despite spectacular scenery, there are no real drops or climbs and no real opportunities to get lost. Relax and enjoy ambience until you arrive at **Coastguard Headquarters** on **St Ann's Head**. The blockhouses and fort along this stretch of coast show how much strategic military importance was placed on **Milford Haven** in the past.

❸ At road, turn **R** and walk along drive, past lookout tower, to gate. Here, coast path veers **L** and then **R**, to

follow series of marker posts along fence towards lighthouse and bank of cottages on R. At cottages, turn sharp **L** to cross green to track that leads behind walled enclosure. This then drops to join coast again above **Mill Bay**.

❹ Drop down to cross head of bay and climb up again to follow field edges around to Beacon on **West Blockhouse Point**. You'll pass pair of dew ponds and then come to crossroads, where you keep ahead.

❺ Path again swings inland, this time to drop down to **Watwick Bay**. Climb away from beach and follow path to **beacon** on **Watwick Point**. After following along edge of another 2 fields, cross stile and drop to **R** to start descent to **Castle Beach**. Cross footbridge and climb up steps towards narrow peninsula of **Dale Fort**. As ground levels, you'll meet junction of paths where you keep straight ahead to road. Turn **L** and follow it down, through woodland, to **Dale** and car park.

# Stackpole Beaches and Lakes

**6 miles (9.7km)** 2hrs 30min **Ascent:** 390ft (119m) ▲

**Paths:** Easy coast path, quiet lanes and well trodden waterside walkways, 1 stile

**Suggested map:** OS Explorer OL36 South Pembrokeshire

**Grid reference:** SR 976938

**Parking:** National Trust car park above Broad Haven Beach

**An undemanding tour of the clifftops, beaches and lakes at the southernmost point of the Pembrokeshire Coast National Park.**

**①** From car park, head back to National Trust building at head of lane and bear **R**, down set of steps, to beach. Cross beach and keep **L** to walk up creek to footbridge.

**②** Go over this and bear **R** to walk above rocky outcrops, above beach, to gate. Follow grassy path around headland and back inland to stile above **Saddle Bay**. Continue around large blowhole and up to gate above deeply cloven zawn (cleft), known as **Raming Hole**.

**③** Go through gate and hug coastline on your **R** to walk around **Stackpole Head**. As you turn back inland, pass blowhole and then go through gate to drop down to **Barafundle Bay**. Cross back of beach and climb up steps on other side to archway in wall. Continue around to **Stackpole Quay**.

**④** Turn **L**, above tiny harbour, to pass Old Boathouse Tearoom on your **L** before turning sharp **R** on to road. Follow this past some buildings on **R** and up to T-junction, where you turn **L**.

**⑤** Drop down into **Stackpole** village, pass **Stackpole Inn** on **R**, and continue around a series of bends until you come to road on **L**, over bridge.

**⑥** Cross bridge and bear **L** to follow good path along side of lake. This leads through 1 kissing gate to 2nd, where you bear **R**, up short steep section. At top, bear **L**, on to broad path with wooden handrail. Follow this to bridge.

**⑦** Don't cross over bridge, but drop down on to path and follow it, keeping lake on your **L**. Continue straight ahead to another bridge, cross it, then carry on with lake now on your **R-H** side. This path leads to footbridge that you crossed at Point **②**. Retrace your steps across beach and up steps back to car park above **Broad Haven Beach**.

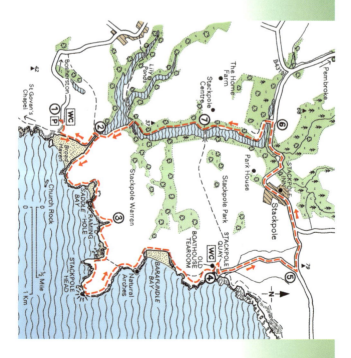

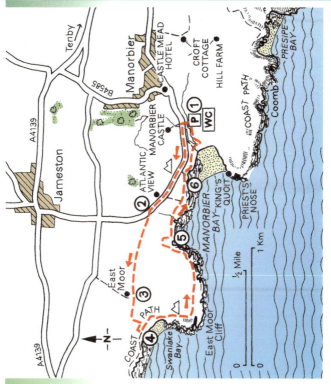

# Manorbier Swanlake Bay

**3 miles (4.8km)** 1hr 30min **Ascent:** 290ft (88m)

**Paths:** Coast path, clear paths across farmland, 6 stiles.

**Suggested map:** OS Explorer OL36 South Pembrokeshire

**Grid reference:** SS 063976

**Parking:** Pay-and-display car park by beach below castle

**Note:** Not suitable for dogs due to difficult stiles

A short stroll across open farmland before taking in a **remote cove** and **some breathtaking coastal scenery.**

❶ Visit the impressive 11th-century **Manorbier Castle** either before or after your walk. Walk out of car park entrance and turn **L** on to narrow lane. Follow lane steeply upwards and bearing around to **R**. You'll continue to climb above coastline and pass impressively situated and well-named **Atlantic View** cottage on your **R** before reaching double gate and stile on your **L**.

❷ Cross stile and walk along field edge, with bank and fence on your **R**, to reach stone step stile. Cross stile and continue heading in same direction to wooden stile, which you also cross. Continue to stone step stile by farmhouse, which brings you into small enclosure, then to wooden stile that leads you away from buildings.

❸ Continue again along edge of field to another stone stile. Cross this stile and turn **L** to drop down field edge to yet another stile that leads on to **coast path.** Access to beach is more or less directly beneath you and this remote and beautiful cove is an excellent spot for a picnic on a sunny day.

❹ Turn **L** on to coast path and follow it over stile and steeply uphill. You'll eventually reach top on a lovely airy ridge that swings east and then north to drop steeply down into narrow dip above **Manorbier Bay.**

❺ Cross over another stile and climb out of dip to continue walking easily above rocky beach. This path leads to drive, beneath large house.

❻ Continue beneath The Dak and uphill slightly, where coast path drops off to **R**. Follow this as it skirts small car park then winds down through gorse and bracken to beach. Cross stream and turn **L** to follow sandy track back to car park.

# Newport Walk with Angels

**5½ miles (8.8km)** 3hrs 30min **Ascent:** 1,080ft (329m) ⛰

**Paths:** Coast footpaths, boggy tracks, rough paths over bracken and heather-covered hillsides, 2 stiles

**Suggested map:** OS Explorer OL35 North Pembrokeshire

**Grid reference:** SN 057392

**Parking:** Free car park opposite information centre, Long Street

---

**Explore Newport then a stiff climb to Carn Ingli, one of Britain's most sacred hilltops.**

**①** Turn **R** out of car park and **L** on to High Street. Fork **L** into Pen y Bont and continue to bridge, where waymarked footpath leads off to **L**. Follow this along banks of estuary to small road.

**②** Turn **R**, walk past toilets to its end, where path follows sea wall. Continue to another lane; turn **L** to follow it to **A487**. Turn **R** on to this road then **L** to continue up drive of **Hendre** farm.

**③** Go through gate, to **L** of buildings, and follow track across small stream. Path hugs **L** edge of field to reach another gate. Maintain direction along hedged section (boggy). Keep straight ahead at stile to climb up to road.

**④** Turn **R** on to road then fork **L** to continue past houses to pair of huge **stones** on **L**. Pass through these stones and follow faint track up to rocky tor. From here, head up towards larger tor of **Carn Ffoi**.

From here you'll be able to pick up clearer path that leads on to broken wall.

**⑤** Pass through it and follow clear footpath across hillside, aiming towards obvious top of **Carn Ingli**, which rises ahead of you. Pass beneath highpoint of **Carningli** Common, where you'll see faint footpath on **R-H** side heading up towards shallow saddle. Take this footpath then, as ground levels off, bear **L** to follow any of faint tracks that lead up on to ridge.

**⑥** Follow ridge line northwards and drop down, again on faint footpaths, to join good, clear track that runs straight down hillside. Continue on this, keeping ahead at 2 crossroads. Turn **L** then **R** when you get to next junction. This drops down to gate in corner, which leads on to lane.

**⑦** Take lane to crossroads and keep ahead to walk past house to obvious sunken track. Follow this down to drive; turn **L**, then **R**, on to Church Street. Continue into centre and cross main road into Long Street.

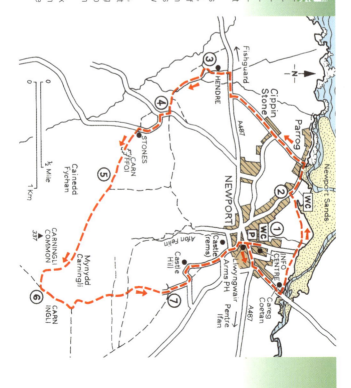

# Rhandirmwyn Dinas Circuit

**2 miles (3.2km)** 1hr **Ascent:** 230ft (70m) ▲

**Paths:** Clearly defined tracks and boardwalks, a few steps

**Suggested map:** OS Explorer 187 Llandovery

**Grid reference:** SN 787471

**Parking:** RSPB Dinas and Gwenffrwd Nature Reserve Visitor Centre, 4 miles (6.4km) north of Rhandirmwyn

**An easy saunter around the rugged scenery of the RSPB Dinas and Gwenffrwd Nature Reserve.**

❶ Walk through kissing gate at far end of car park and follow boardwalk easily across open ground. It dips slightly to cross over boggy forest floor, where trees are home to countless nest boxes, and then rises again to enter woodland properly. Boardwalk comes to end at fork at bottom of wood.

❷ Turn **L** and follow slightly higher of 2 obvious tracks. This contours through oak trees, dropping close to fence on L. Another track comes in from road on L but keep above this and continue through forest, trending rightwards all the time.

❸ You're now walking parallel to **Afon Tywi.** Continue beneath some impressive crags to bench at great vantage point above its turbulent confluence

with Afon Doethie. Path drops to bank of river, where it offers great views over rapids. Continue upstream, path winds contorted route around and over few large boulders. As you reach distinct meander of river, you'll notice birch and rowan trees as well as oak. There's another bench above meander and this offers great views of crags on opposing hillside.

❹ Path then drops again to follow river to open ground, where you keep slightly **R**. The going eases now as you follow grassy path towards small stand of birch trees, where there's another bench – this one uniquely hewn out of twisted branches. Climb easily up for few yards (metres) and then continue to end of boardwalk. Turn **L** to follow this back to car park.

# Pumlumon Remote Lake

**5½ miles (8.8km)** 3hrs **Ascent:** 623ft (190m)

**Paths:** Good track up, sketchy return path

**Suggested map:** OS Explorer 213 Aberystwyth & Cwm Rheidol

**Grid reference:** SN 762861

**Parking:** Off-road parking – there is room for several cars by woods at start of walk, alternatively use car park by Nant-y-moch dam

**Discover a tarn set among the rocks of the Rheidol's dark northern corrie.**

❶ From car parking spaces beneath woods east of Nant-y-moch dam (near spot height 392m on OS Explorer maps), walk north along road and take **R-H** fork. The road descends to cross streams of **Nant Maesant-fach** and **Nant-y-moch** before traversing rough moorland along east shores of **Nant-y-moch Reservoir.** The reservoir, stocked with native brown trout, is popular with anglers during season.

❷ Beneath quarried rocks of **Bryn y Beddau,** rubble track on **R-H** side of road doubles back up hillside then swings round to **L.** The steep sides of **Pumlumon** now soar away to skyline on your **R,** with little stream of Maesant tumbling down them. The track climbs further, then levels out to pass some shallow lakes, which lie above rocks of **Fainc Ddu uchaf.** Now high above bare valleys of Hyddgen and Hengwm, track

swings south beneath crags of **Pumlumon Fach** to arrive at **Llyn Llygad Rheidol's** dam.

❸ To get to footpath along other side you'll have to ford stream short way downhill – take care if stream is in spate. Path, which runs parallel to eastern banks of stream, is sketchy in places, especially where you ford side stream. It descends peaty terrain where mosses and moor grasses proliferate.

❹ When you reach small stand of conifers in Hengwm Valley, turn **L** to follow old cart track which fords Afon Rheidol, close to its confluence with Afon Hengwm. Track heads west and soon Hengwm Valley meets that of Afon Hyddgen. Track swings southwest and passes between squat cliffs of **Fainc Ddu uchaf** and western shores of **Nant-y-moch Reservoir.**

❺ Go through gate above outdoor adventure centre at **Maesant** and continue along tarmac lane used in outward route, to return to car park.

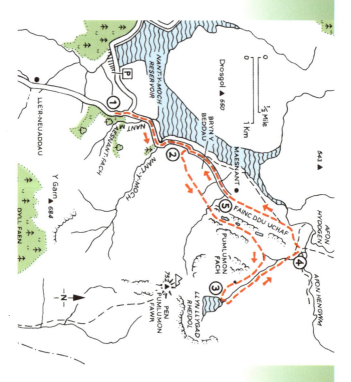

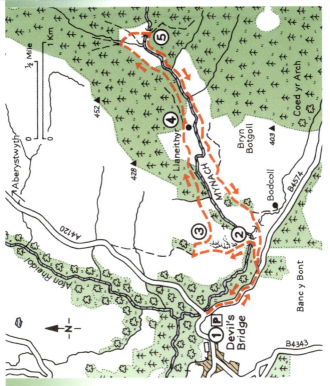

# Devil's Bridge Mynach River Ramble

**5½ miles (8.8km)** 2hrs 30min **Ascent:** 525ft (160m) ▲

**Paths:** Mainly clearly defined tracks across open ground and through forests – riverside sections can be boggy, 8 stiles

**Suggested map:** OS Explorer 213 Aberystwyth & Cwm Rheidol

**Grid reference:** SN 742768

**Parking:** Large car park on the B4574, Cwm Ystwyth road, out of Devil's Bridge

An easy riverside circuit from the enchanting village of Devil's Bridge. The bridge dates from the 12th century and together with the spectacular waterfalls is one of the most popular tourist attractions in Wales.

❶ Turn **R** out of car park and walk along road to waymarked bridleway on your **L**. Go through gate and turn immediately **L** on to narrow footpath that drops down to river. Cross over bridge and walk up other side to stile.

❷ Keep straight ahead, with some rocky hills to your **R**, to another stile. Cross this and follow track to waymark post. Turn **R** and climb past another post to good track. Cross this and turn **R** to traverse hillside, in wood, to another post on grassy shoulder.

❸ Keep straight ahead to another post and then drop to contour around gorse-covered hillside. Continue to stream and stile, which you cross to enter

plantation. Continue to another stile and drop to meet good track. Keep **L** on to this and follow it above grand-looking house to fork above some ruined buildings.

❹ Fork **R** and follow good track along above **Mynach river**. Eventually it bends leftwards to follow above banks of tributary. Shortly after this, waymark directs you **R**, down some steps and over tributary. Keep straight ahead to post by small bank. Turn **R** here and drop down to bridge over **Mynach**.

❺ Turn **R** to follow path downstream. Continue, through succession of gates, to gate on **L** that leads on to clear track. Follow this, away from river and up to join another good track. Turn **R** on to this and follow it to fork where you turn **R** through gate. Continue around hillside and over footbridge. Climb up past house and continue to **B4574**. Turn **R** to drop down to car park.

# Neuadd Reservoirs In the Brecon Beacons

**7½ miles (12.1km)** 4hrs **Ascent:** 2,000ft (610m) ▲

**Paths:** Clear well-trodden paths, small boggy patches, broad rocky track; 1 stile

**Suggested map:** OS Explorer OL12 Brecon Beacons National Park Western & Central areas

**Grid reference:** SO 032179

**Parking:** At end of small lane leading north from Pontsticill

**A magical tour of reservoirs, high ridges and mountains.**

**❶** Continue up lane to small gate, which leads into grounds of **reservoir**. Keep walking ahead to drop down narrow path to concrete bridge across outflow. Cross bridge and climb up on to bank opposite where you bear **L** to walk along top of bank. This will take you to gate that leads out on to open moorland.

**❷** Go through this and keep ahead, taking **L-H** of 2 tracks, which leads easily uphill towards edge of mainly felled forest. Follow clear track up, with forest to your **L**, and then climb steeply up stony gully to top of escarpment.

**❸** Once there, turn **R** on to obvious path and follow escarpment for over 2½ miles (4km). You'll eventually drop into distinct saddle with flat-topped summit of **Corn Du** directly ahead. Where path forks, keep ahead and climb easily up on to summit. Follow escarpment edge along then drop down into another saddle, where

you take path up on to next peak, **Pen y Fan**.

**❹** Again, from summit cairn, follow escarpment around and drop steeply, on rocky path, down into deep col beneath **Cribyn**. Keep ahead to climb steeply up to cairn on narrow summit. Note: this climb can be avoided by forking **R** and following another clear path that contours **R** around southern flanks of mountain and brings you out at Point **❻**.

**❺** From top, bear slightly **R** and follow escarpment around to southeast. After long flat stretch, drop steeply down into deep col, **Bwlch ar y Fan**.

**❻** Cross stile and turn **R** on to well-made track that leads easily down mountain. Follow this for over 1½ miles (2.4km), until it starts to swing slightly to **L** and drops steeply into rocky ravine. Turn **R** here on to track and take it down to beck. Go through this, turn **L** and follow track to its end. Turn **R** on to another track that leads back to head of lane. Go through gate and follow lane back to your car.

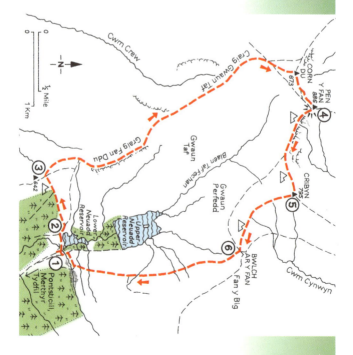

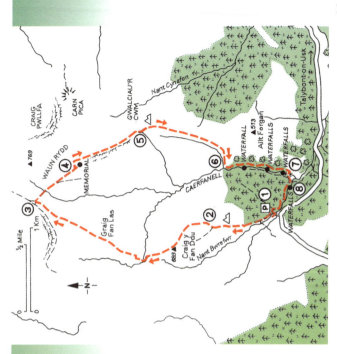

# Caerfanell Valley Skyline Walking

5½ miles **(8.8km)** 3hrs 30min **Ascent:** 1,542ft (470m) ⚑

**Paths:** Clear tracks across mountain tops, river and forest paths, some mud and wet peat, 3 stiles

**Suggested map:** OS Explorer OL12 Brecon Beacons National Park Western & Central areas

**Grid reference:** SO 056175

**Parking:** Large car park at start, 3 miles (4.8km) west of Talybont Reservoir

**Spectacular escarpments above a wild and remote valley.**

**1** Walk back out of car park, either crossing cattle grid or stile to **L**. Turn immediately **R** on to stone track that heads uphill, with stream on your **L**. Follow this track steeply up to top of escarpment and keep ahead to cross narrow spur, where you bear around, slightly **L**, to follow escarpment.

**2** Stay on clear path, with escarpment to your **R**, for about 1½ miles (2.4km), until you meet a number of paths at head of valley.

**3** Turn **R** to follow narrow track slightly downwards, around head of valley, towards cliffs that can be seen on opposite hillside. Keep **L** at fork and continue to **memorial**, which marks where a Wellington bomber R1645 crashed, killing its Canadian crew, in 1942.

**4** Almost directly above **memorial**, you'll see rocky gully leading up on to ridge. On **L-H** side of this, as you look at it, is faint track that climbs steeply up. Take this

to top; turn **R** on to narrow but clear track. Follow this track above crag, to distinctive cairn at southern end of ridge. Just north of cairn you'll see small stream.

**5** Follow this down for 10ft (3m) to join clear grassy track that trends towards **L** at first, then follows clear grove down spur. This becomes easy footpath that crosses broad plateau then leads to junction at a wall. Turn **R** here and drop down to **Caerfanell river.**

**6** Cross stile on your **L** at bottom and follow narrow footpath downstream, past **waterfalls**. Eventually you'll pass largest of them and come to footbridge.

**7** Cross footbridge then stile to follow track into forest. Pass ruined buildings on your **R**, and before you cross small bridge, turn **R** on to clear path that leads uphill into forest with **waterfalls** on your **L**.

**8** Continue uphill on main track, taking optional detours to **L** and **R** to see other waterfalls. Eventually you'll meet broader forest track where you turn **L** then **R** to return to car park.

# Porth yr ogof Along the Waterfalls

**4 miles (6.4km)** 2hrs **Ascent:** 360ft (110m) ⚠

**Paths:** Riverside paths, some rough sections and steps, no stiles

**Suggested map:** OS Explorer OL12 Brecon Beacons National Park Western & Central areas

**Grid reference:** SN 928124

**Parking:** Park car park at Porth yr ogof, near Ystradfellte

## Riverside scenery and four waterfalls.

❶ Cross over road at entrance to car park and head down **L-H** of 2 paths, waymarked with yellow arrow. Follow this path on to river bank, then keep river to your **R** to follow rough footpath through 2 kissing gates to reach footbridge.

❷ Continue ahead, drop into dip and climb steeply out. Keep **L** to climb to broken wall where path forks. Take **L** fork here (bottom **R-H** path has fence along it) and follow edge of wood. When you see odd green-banded marker posts, follow them to waymarked crossroads where you turn **R**, now following red-banded posts.

❸ Continue through dark tunnel of trees and out into more evenly spaced deciduous woodland. Carry on following waymarked trail to post directing you downhill. Follow this track and then bear around to **R** when you reach edge of forest. This leads to top of set of wooden steps, on **L**.

❹ Go down steps to **Sgwd yr Eira** (Waterfall of the Snow) and then, having edged along bank and walked behind falls (waterproofs are recommended), retrace your steps back to edge of the wood. Turn **L** and continue, still following red-banded posts, to fork marked with green-banded post.

❺ Turn **L** and descend to riverside. Turn **L** again to **Sgwd y Pannwr** (Fullers Falls) and then turn around to walk upstream to **Sgwd Isaf Clun-Gwyn** (Lower Waterfall of the White Meadow). Take care here, as ground is very steep and rough around best viewpoint.

❻ Retrace your steps downstream to your descent path and turn **L** to climb back up to fork at top. Turn **L** and follow red-banded waymarkers along to **Sgwd Clun-gwyn**, where there's a fenced-off viewing area. From here, continue along main trail to place where you split off earlier.

❼ Keep to **L-H** side to drop into dip and retrace your steps past footbridge and back to **Porth yr ogof**.

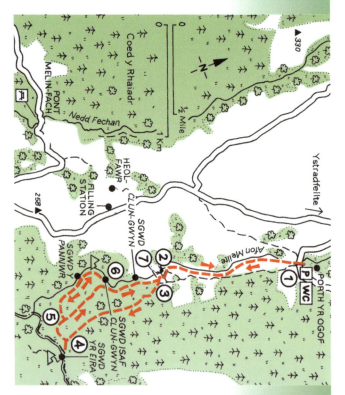

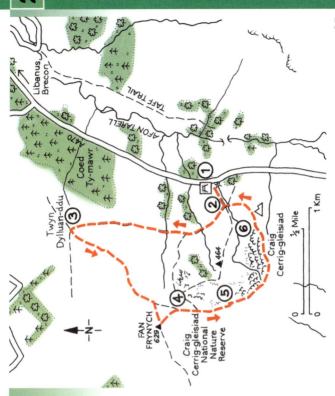

# Craig Cerrig-gleisiad Back to Nature

**4 miles (6.4km)** 2hrs **Ascent:** 1,050ft (320m)

**Paths:** Clear footpaths and broad stony tracks, 4 stiles

**Suggested map:** OS Explorer OL12 Brecon Beacons National Park Western & Central areas

**Grid reference:** SN 972221

**Parking:** Pull-in by small picnic area on A470, 2 miles (3.2km) north of Storey Arms

**The formidable crags of one of the Beacon's best-known nature reserves.**

**1** This is one of many possible walks in the large 156-acre (63ha) National Nature reserve but it is the closest (in this collection) to the National Park Visitor Centre on Mynydd Illtud Common, near Libanus. It is a great source of information about the National Park and hosts some great displays and has a programme of guided walks. There is a bridge and a small picnic area at southern end of lay-by. Walk towards this and go through adjacent signposted kissing gate (**'Twyn Dylluan-ddu** and Forest Lodge'). Head towards crags, following clear footpath, until you come to gap in next wall.

**2** Pass through this and turn **R** to follow dry-stone wall north. Head down into small valley, cross stream, then stile to continue in same direction. Drop into another, steeper, valley and climb out, still following track. Continue through bracken to stile.

**3** Cross and turn **L** on to stony track. Follow this up to gate and stile and continue through rough ground, churned up by mining, until it levels on dished plateau. Bear **R** here to whitewashed trig point of **Fan Frynych**, then turn sharp **L** to return to main track above escarpment.

**4** Turn **R** on to main track again and continue past more rough ground before dropping slightly into broad but shallow valley. At bottom, go over stile by gate.

**5** Cross another stile on your **L** and turn **R** to continue in same direction, this time with fence to your **R**. Climb up to highest point, then follow obvious path around top of cliffs. Path starts to drop, easily at first but getting steeper as you go.

**6** Continue carefully down steep section and follow path around to **L** when you reach easier ground. This leads you to stream, which you can ford or jump (it's narrower a few paces downstream). Turn **R**, through gap in wall, and follow outward path back to car park.

# Pen y Fan The Beacons Horseshoe

**7 miles (11.3km) 4hrs Ascent** 2,100ft (640m) ⛰

**Paths:** Well-defined paths and tracks, short distance on quiet lanes, 4 stiles

**Suggested map:** OS Explorer OL12 Brecon Beacons National Park Western & Central areas

**Grid reference:** SO 025248

**Parking:** Car park at end of small lane, 3 miles (4.8km) south of Brecon

**The connoisseur's way up to the high ground.**

❶ Walk uphill from car park and pass information plinth before crossing stile. Walk along **R-H** side of field to top **R-H** corner and then bear **L** to continue along fence to another stile.

❷ Follow broad but faint grassy track straight on. It gradually becomes a better-defined stony track that swings slightly **L** and climbs hillside. Continue ahead, up towards head of **Cwm Gwdi**, and keep ahead, ignoring few R forks, until path eventually levels out on **Cefn Cwm Llwch**.

❸ Continue along ridge towards summit ahead. As you reach foot of peak, track steepens considerably, offering views over a perilous gully that drops into **Cwm Sere** on **L**. Continue to climb steeply over few rocky steps to reach summit cairn on **Pen y Fan**.

❹ Bear **R** to follow escarpment edge along and drop into shallow saddle beneath rising crest of **Corn Du**. Continue up on to this summit, then bear **L** to drop

down through rocky outcrops on to easier ground below. Bear sharp **R** once you reach grassy hillside to walk north beneath peak.

❺ Continue down hill and pass Tommy Jones **obelisk** with steep crags of **Craig Cwm Llwch** on your R-H side. Above lake, path forks; take **R-H** option and drop steeply, around dog-leg and over moraine banks to lake shore.

❻ A clear track leads north from lake; follow it over easy ground to cross wall that leads on to broad farm track. Take this down to gate in front of building and climb stile on **L**. Cross compound and climb another stile to follow waymarker posts around to **R** on to another track, beyond building.

❼ Bear **L** on to this track and follow it down, over footbridge, to parking area. Keep ahead through gate to T-junction, where you turn **R**. Cross over bridge and continue for over 1 mile (1.6km) to another T-junction. Turn **R** and walk uphill back to car park.

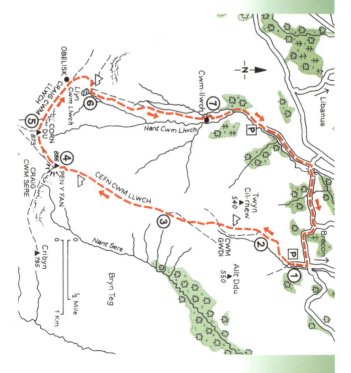

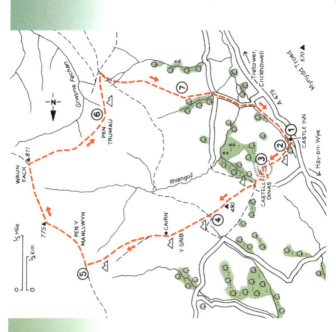

# Y Grib An Airy Stroll

**8 miles (12.9km)** 4hrs 30min **Ascent:** 1,960ft (597m) ▲

**Paths:** Clear tracks over farmland, rolling moorland and narrow ridge, quiet lane, 3 stiles

**Suggested map:** OS Explorer OL13 Brecon Beacons National Park Eastern area

**Grid reference:** SO 175295

**Parking:** Castle Inn, Pengenffordd, allows parking for small fee

A strenuous climb on to the Black Mountains via one of the Beacon's finest ridges.

**1** Wooden steps go down from back of car park on eastern side of road. These lead on to rough track where you turn **R** then immediately **L** over stile. Follow permissive path down side of wood to stream, cross it and clamber over another stile.

**2** Keep to **L** edge of field, with wood on your **L**, and climb steeply to top of field. Leave wood behind and follow fence line upwards to another stile. This leads on to flanks of **Castell Dinas**.

**3** Keep ahead here to cross over ruins and descend steeply into deep saddle. Cross over broad track and then climb directly up steep spur ahead. You are now on **Y Grib** and it's possible to follow faint track all the way up to **cairn** then down to small notch where your route is crossed by bridleway.

**4** Climb steeply back out of this and hug crest up to another **cairn**, where ridge joins main escarpment.

Don't be drawn off to **L**; instead keep ahead to climb short steep wall on to broad spur of **Pen y Manllwyn**, where you'll meet clear track.

**5** Turn **R** on to this track; follow it up to boggy plateau on top of **Waun Fach**. Summit is marked by concrete block that used to act as base for trig point. Turn **R**; follow obvious path down on to ever-narrowing spur of **Pen Trumau**.

**6** Cross narrow summit and, as ground steepens, follow path through rocky outcrops to broad saddle. Turn sharp **R** here; follow main track as it descends, easily at first. This steepens and becomes rocky for a while before it reaches gate above walled track.

**7** Follow track down to road; turn **R**, then immediately **L**. Drop to bottom of valley and climb out again on other side. As road turns sharply to **L**, bear **R** on to stony farm track that runs between hedgerows. Follow this track past stile you crossed earlier, on R-H side, then take steps on your **L**, back to car park.

# Pen Cerrig-calch The Crickhowell Skyline

**Paths:** Waymarked footpaths, clear tracks, 8 stiles

**8½ miles (13.7km)** 4hrs 30min **Ascent:** 1,700ft (518m) ▲

**Suggested map:** OS Explorer OL13 Brecon Beacons National Park Eastern area

**Grid reference:** SO 234228

**Parking:** Car park beneath small crag and next to bridge, in narrow lane running north from Crickhowell

## Views of Crickhowell and the remote valleys of the central Black Mountains.

**1** Walk back over bridge and up ramp that leads to 2nd gate on **R**. Cross stile and walk up edge of field to another stile that leads on to lane. Cross this and climb over another stile to continue, with wood on your **L**, up to yet another stile in dry-stone wall.

**2** Cross this and turn **L** to follow faint path around hillside through bracken. Walk alongside wall, at one stage dropping slightly, and then, as wall drops to **L** in open area, turn **R** to climb slightly to another fork beneath steep bank. Keep **L** here to join wall again.

**3** Continue for about 500yds (457m) to another open spot where wall dips to **L** and turn **R** on to track that leads up on to summit of **Table Mountain**.

**4** Turn off plateau at its narrowest northern point and cross saddle on obvious track. This climbs steeply up on to **Pen Cerrig-calch**. As path levels, ignore track to **L** and keep ahead until you reach trig point.

**5** Continue ahead to drop slightly down small crag to meet escarpment edge. Continue along ridge, which narrows slightly, then climb again to narrow summit of **Pen Allt-mawr**.

**6** A path leads down steep northern spur. Take this and cross flat, open and often wet ground towards small hump ahead. As you start to climb, you'll come to parting of paths.

**7** Fork **R** here and continue to small **cairn** on top of narrow ridge that leads southwest. Follow ridge easily down until you cross some quarried ground and come to large **cairn**. Walk down to stile at top of plantation. Cross this and then follow rutted track down to another stile.

**8** This leads on to sunken track, which you follow downhill to junction of paths. Keep half **R** to cross stile and head along top of field to marker post that sends you **L**, downhill. Bear **L** at bottom of field by gate. This leads back to car park.

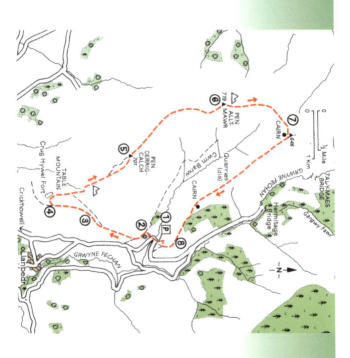

# Montgomery Marcher Lords Land

4½ miles (7.2km) 2hrs 30min **Ascent:** 853ft (260m) ▲▲

**Paths:** Well-defined paths, farm tracks and country lanes, 3 stiles

**Suggested map:** OS Explorer 216 Welshpool & Montgomery

**Grid reference:** SJ 224963

**Parking:** Car park on Bishops Castle Street on B4385 at south end of town

**Iron-Age and medieval castles and views across a wide landscape.**

**1** Montgomery is a fine country town with its origins in medieval times. Tucked beneath a castle-topped crag, many of the houses have Georgian façades but these are additions to older dwellings and the town is definitely worth exploring. From car park head north, then **L** along Broad Street, where you'll see **Dragon Hotel** and **town hall**. A signpost points to lane up to **castle** – a must see and free. Retrace your steps to **town hall** and head north up Arthur Street, past **Old Bell Museum**, and join main road, Princes Street.

**2** Continue north, ignoring turn for Chirbury, then turn **L** out of town along Station Road, B4385. Ignore 1st footpath on **L** side of road, but go over stile and cross field at 2nd stile. Path climbs through woodland, then swings **L** (southwest) to reach old hilltop fort above Ffridd Faldwyn.

**3** Go over stile at far side of fort and descend across more fields to roadside gate. Turn **L** down road, which takes you back towards **Montgomery**.

**4** As road turns sharp R just above town, leave it for footpath on **R** ('Montgomeryshire War Memorial') beginning beyond kissing gate. Footpath climbs steadily up hill to join farm track, which runs parallel to **Town Ditch** at first.

**5** As it enters high pastures, track begins to level out and traverse eastern hillside. Here you can detour to **war memorial** that lies clearly ahead at top of hill. Return to track and follow it through gate and past some pens with gorse and hawthorn lining way on L.

**6** In field above **Castell-y-gwynt farm**, on R-H side of path, footpath turns **R** to follow hedge. Go over stile at far side of field and turn **L** along a farm lane that descends to join narrow tarmac country lane southwest of **Little Mount** farm. Turn **L** along this.

**7** Turn **L** at 1st T-junction and **L** at 2nd. Follow lane back into **Montgomery**.

# Powis Castle The Montgomery Canal

**4 miles (6.4km)** **Ascent:** 262ft (80m) ▲

**Paths:** Tarmac drive, field path, canal tow path, 3 stiles

**Suggested map:** OS Explorer 216 Welshpool & Montgomery

**Grid reference:** SJ 226075

**Parking:** Large pay car park off Church Street, Welshpool

**See how the Earls of Powis lived as you walk through their deer park and past their huge red palace on the hill.**

**❶** From main car park, pass **tourist information centre** then go **L** along Church Street. At crossroads in centre of town turn **R** up Broad Street, which later becomes High Street.

**❷** Just beyond **town hall** turn **L** past small car parking area and then pass through impressive wrought iron gates of **Powis Castle Estate**. Now follow tarmac drive through park grounds and past **Llyn Du** (black lake).

**❸** Take **R** fork, high road, which leads to north side of castle. You can detour from the walk here to visit the world-famous gardens and castle with its fine paintings and furniture and works of Indian art collected by Robert Clive. Continue on walk on high road and follow it past 2 more pools on **L** and **Ladies Pool** on **R** to reach country lane.

**❹** Turn **L** along lane. Opposite next estate entrance leave lane for path on **R** which follows dirt track across field. Track turns **L** over bridge and into another field. Here you follow fence on **R** and cut diagonally across fields to step stile in far corner. Over this, clear sunken grass track continues across another field to reach country lane close to **Montgomery Canal**. It was built by three different companies and was opened in stages from 1796. The canal is gradually being restored and you may see narrowboats cruising along this section.

**❺** Turn **L** along lane before taking a path on **L** which descends to canal tow path at **Belan Locks**. Head north along canal, passing close to some half-timbered cottages. Pass **Powysland Museum and Canal Centre**, with its exhibits of local agriculture and crafts and canal and railway systems, to reach wharf and aqueduct at Welshpool. Turn **L** here along tarred path to return to car park.

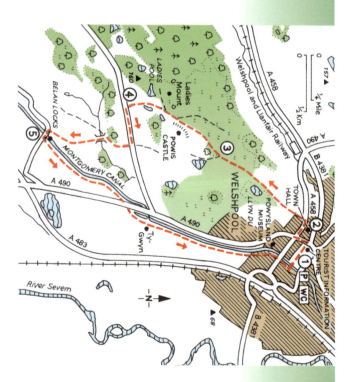

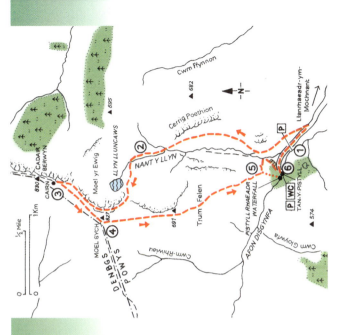

# Pistyll Rhaeadr And Cadair Berwyn

**5 miles (8km)** 3hrs **Ascent:** 1,870ft (570m) ⚠

**Paths:** Well-defined paths and tracks, 6 stiles

**Suggested map:** OS Explorer 255 Llangollen & Berwyn

**Grid reference:** SJ 076293

**Parking:** Car park 220yds (201m) before Tan-y-pistyll farm/café, where there's another pay car park

**This demanding, but short, walk brings magnificent views and spectacular falls.**

❶ From more easterly, and smaller, of 2 car parks turn **R** along road for 400yds (366m), then go through farm gate to follow wide grassy track that climbs northwest to enter cwm of **Nant y Llyn**. Here track heads north towards crags of **Cerrig Poethion**. Ignore path down to sheepfold by banks of stream below.

❷ The track degenerates into path that traverses hillsides scattered with gorse. Higher up it fords 2 outlet streams of **Llyn Lluncaws** before reaching moss and heather cwm of tarn. Now path climbs south of lake and up shale and grass spur to base of **Moel Sych's** crags. Follow path along edge of crags on **R** to reach col between **Moel Sych** and **Cadair Berwyn**. From here climb to rocky south top of latter peak. The trip to trig point on Cadair Berwyn's lower north summit is straightforward but offers no advantages as a viewpoint.

❸ From south top retrace your footsteps to col, but this time instead of tracing cliff edge follow ridge fence to cairn on Moel Sych summit plateau.

❹ Waymarker by summit ladder stile points way south, descending across wide, peaty spur with moor grass, mosses and heather. Note path follows west side of fence, not east shown on current maps. Halfway down cross stile and follow east side of fence. Beyond 2nd stile path descends southeast into high moorland cwm of **Disgynfa**, where path is met by stony track that has climbed from base of falls.

❺ To make there-and-back detour to top of falls, ignore stony track, and instead go through gate into forest and follow path to river. If not, descend along previously mentioned track, which zig-zags down before turning **R** to head for **Tan-y-pistyll** complex. Path to bottom of falls starting from café leads to footbridge across Afon Rhaeadr for best views.

❻ From café walk along road to car park.

# Central Brecon Beacons Cwm Cynwyn

**9½ miles (15.3km)** 5hrs 30min **Ascent:** 2,360ft (719m) ▲

**Paths:** Mostly clear paths along broad grassy ridges, 3 stiles

**Suggested map:** OS Outdoor Leisure 12 Brecon Beacons National Park

**Grid reference:** SH 039244

**Parking:** At Pont y Caniedydd and a few spaces at the head of the road

**This walk follows airy ridges to some of the lesser-visited peaks of the Brecon Beacons.**

**①** Cross bridge and climb steeply up road past **Bailea** on your L. Keep straight ahead at junction where road levels and follow stony track up to gate that leads on to open ground by a National Trust sign.

**②** Continue straight up track and then fork **R**, over stile, to climb more steeply on to crest of grassy ridge. Follow ridge along and then climb steeply up sharp snout of **Cribyn**. Bear **L** at summit and follow escarpment edge along, dropping steeply down into **Bwlch ar y Fan.**

**③** Cross track in saddle and climb steeply up hillside opposite. Bear around to **L** at top and continue up summit of **Fan y Big.** Keep ahead in same direction to drop steeply down broad grassy ridge. The going eases for a while, steepens for a short distance and then eases again. Continue until path drops steeply once more, to edge of open ground.

**④** Bear **L,** towards bottom, and follow path as it contours around hillside above wall. After short spell of walking alongside wall, it drops away to your **R.** Continue traversing until you see **ruined building** down to your **R.** Cross stile here and follow track down around bend by ruin. Continue to stream, which you ford.

**⑤** Climb up other side and turn **R** on to good track. Follow this into farmyard and turn **L,** through gate, on to grassy track. Continue upward to another gate, which leads out on to open ground at foot of **Cwmcynwyn.** Turn **R** and follow track back down to start and parking place.

42

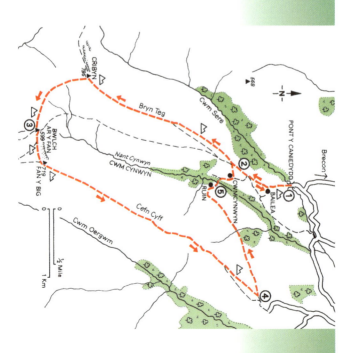

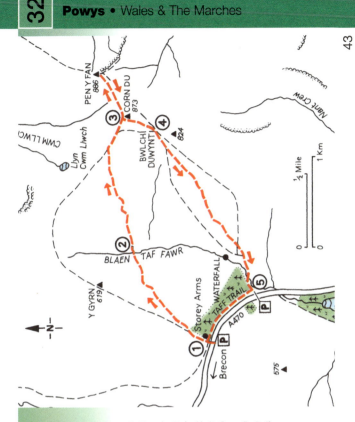

# Central Brecon Beacons Pen Y Fan Pilgrimage

**5 miles (8km)** 2hrs 30min **Ascent:** 1,610ft (491m) ▲

**Paths:** Clearly defined tracks

**Suggested map:** OS Outdoor Leisure 12 Brecon Beacons National Park

**Grid reference:** SN 983203

**Parking:** Huge lay-by on the A470, opposite the Storey Arms and a public telephone box

A straightforward circuit that follows the main trade routes up on to the roof of the National Park.

**①** Cross over road and hop over stile next to telephone box. Follow clear, in places man-made, path up hillside, leaving plantation behind and crossing open moorland on southern flanks of **Y Gyrn** – rounded summit to your L. You'll soon gain ridge where you cross stile to drop easily down to infant **Taf Fawr river.**

**②** Continue up other side of valley and keep straight ahead until you reach escarpment edge above **Cwm Llwch.** Turn **R** to follow clear path upward to rocky summit plateau of **Corn Du.** Path slips easily around craggy outcrops on your L and leads you up to huge summit cairn.

**③** Route to **Pen Y Fan** is obvious from here. Drop into shallow saddle and continue easily on to summit. From here, you should have fine views of the Malvern Hills, the Bristol Channel and South Wales. From huge cairn, retrace your steps back across Corn Du to **Bwlch Duwynt,** obvious saddle between summit of Corn Du and long ridge that runs south.

**④** Take main track downhill to **R,** ignoring another track that comes in from R. Follow track easily down for just over 1 mile (1.6km) until you see **Taf Fawr river** to your R. A short diversion will expose a great rocky picnic spot above a small **waterfall.** Continue down to ford river and go through kissing gate into main car park.

**⑤** Turn **R** into car park and follow it to its end where gravel footpath (signposted with **Taff Trail** waymark) takes over. Continue along side of plantation and cross road to return to start.

# Cadair Idris Cwm Cau Horseshoe

**6½ miles (10.4km)** 4hrs 30min **Ascent** 3,120ft (950m) ▲

**Paths:** Mostly clear rocky tracks, some are quite exposed, 6 stiles

**Suggested map:** OS Outdoor Leisure 23 Snowdonia; Cadair Idris

**Grid reference:** SH 732115

**Parking:** Large car park at the start

A rocky ramble to the summit of Cadair Idris **via one of Wales's most beautiful cwms.**

**①** Turn **R** out of car park on to road, and walk for 300 yards (274m) to gates of **Minfford Estate.** Turn **R** through these and follow tree-lined path upwards to gate that leads into **Nature Reserve.** Continue steeply up through wood, with gushing **Nant Cadair** to your **R.** Eventually you'll pass through another gate and out on to open ground by banks of stream.

**②** Don't cross over stream, but instead continue up its west bank and follow path around to **L,** beneath rocky ridge. When path splits, fork **L** (straight ahead to lake shore) and then climb steeply up on to ridge. Bear around to **R** at top and follow cliff line upward to step stile on summit of **Mynydd Pencoed.**

**③** Cross over stile and drop down, still following cliff line, into broad saddle. Continue upwards again, on well cairned path that leads directly to trig point atop **Penygadair's** summit. Drop down from summit to

east (effectively straight ahead) and follow northern escarpment along, over 1 small summit, to 2nd highpoint of **Mynydd Moel,** where you will find small stone shelter.

**④** Turn **R** here (path's quite faint) and drop down grassy spur. As gradient increases, path becomes clearer, crossing stile and winding easily down heather-covered hillside. This eventually leads to **Nant Cadair,** which you cross to rejoin outward path.

**⑤** Turn **L** and retrace your earlier footsteps back down through wood. Instead of returning all way to the road, as you leave woods turn **L,** and follow waymarked track back to car park.

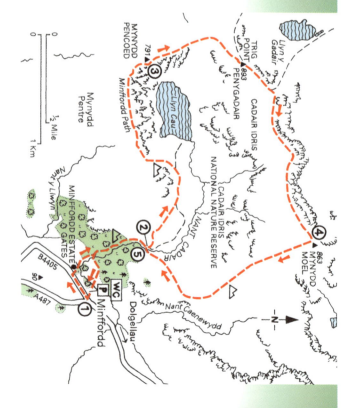

# Llanstumdwy Lloyd George Country

**6 miles (9.7km)** **Ascent:** Negligible ⛰

**Paths:** Generally well-defined paths and tracks, 6 stiles

**Suggested map:** OS Explorer 254 Lleyn Peninsular East

**Grid reference:** SH 476383

**Parking:** Large car park at east end of village

**Note:** Small section of coast path is engulfed by high tides. Check times of tides before setting off

**Following the last Liberal Prime Minister.**

❶ Turn **R** out of car park and go through Llanstumdwy, past **museum** to bridge over **Afon Dwyfor**. Turn **R** along lane, then follow footpath on **L** past **memorial** and down to wooded river banks.

❷ After 2 miles (3.2km) path turns **R**, then tucks under stone archway to meet tarred drive to **Trefan Hall**. Turn **L** along this, continue to **B4411** and turn **R**.

❸ Turn **R** down enclosed drive ('To **Criccieth**'). As another drive merges from L, turn half **L** along path shaded by rhododendrons. After few paces, go through kissing gate, then cross field guided by fence on L. Go through another kissing gate path veers half **R**, following fence now on R.

❹ Beyond another gate, now sketchy route cuts diagonally (southeast) across 2 fields to rejoin **B4411** just 1 mile (1.6km) north of **Criccieth**. Follow **B4411** into town. Keep straight on at crossroads, with main

street, to reach promenade east of **castle**.

❺ Follow coast road as it climbs past **castle** and bears **R** towards railway line. Take bridleway parallel to railway past Muriau, followed by footpath to track north of **Cefn Castell**. Here turn **R**, nearly to railway, then **L** back to coast, east of **Ynysgain Fawr** farm. Follow coast path west along grasslands and gorse scrub to estuary of **Dwyfor**, past crumbled sea defences. Alternatively, if open, pick up coast path from **Criccieth**, without diversions inland. At low tide you can go along sands.

❻ At ladder stile follow wall back towards **Llanystumdwy**. The route becomes farm track that cuts under railway and passes through yard of **Aberkin** farm before reaching main road.

❼ Cross main road with care and go through gate opposite. Short path leads to unsurfaced lane to village centre. Turn **R** for car park.

# Cnicht Tackling the Knight

**6½ miles (10.4km)** 4hrs **Ascent:** 2,297ft (700m) ▲

**Paths:** Mostly well-defined, but sketchy by Bwlch y Battel, 9 stiles

**Suggested map:** OS Explorer OL17 Snowdon

**Grid reference:** SH 631484

**Parking:** Limited roadside parking at Gelli-lago; car park 1 mile (1.6km) to south (grid ref SH 620467)

**An exhilarating climb to one of the peaks.**

**①** If you couldn't park at start of walk, you'll need to walk north from car park for about 1 mile (1.6km) up road before turning **R**, along track to **Gelli-lago** (cottage). Go through gate to **R** of farmhouse, then go through another gate on to footbridge across stream. Gravel path winds up hillside with stream on **L** and **Cnicht** on horizon ahead.

**②** Beyond ladder stile in cross-wall, path veers to **R**, climbing to wild pass of **Bwlch y Battel**. Path peters out, but stay on marshy route between high rocky hillsides. Keep to **L** of tarn, which lies just other side of pass. Soon well-defined track begins and runs alongside foot of **Cnicht's** south ridge to reach and join main Croesor to **Cnicht** route.

**③** Here double-back along path climbing along crest of **Cnicht's** south ridge. On nearing top path divides, both routes reach summit after weaving between rocks.

**④** Continue, passing **Llyn Biswail** on **L** and **Llyn Cwm-y-foel** on **R**, to reach cairn on col overlooking **Llyn yr Adar**.

**⑤** Descend **L** (north) to traverse marshy grasslands to east of large tarn, **Llyn yr Adar**. Path veers northwest beyond northern shores before veering north and following grassy shelf in rocks of Y Cyrniau.

**⑥** At natural grassy dry hollow, path turns sharp **L** to descend westwards towards **Llyn Llagi** – almost circular tarn. Beyond it path traverses rough pastures studded with heather, rock, crumbling walls and occasional tree. It stays roughly parallel to outflow stream of Llyn Llagi.

**⑦** After going over stile and passing to **R** of **Llwynyrhwch** farm, which is surrounded by oak and rhododendron, take path leading across fields to Nantmor road. Turn **L** along road, and pass old converted chapel. If you couldn't park near Gelli-lago, you'll have to continue for 1 mile (1.6km) to car park.

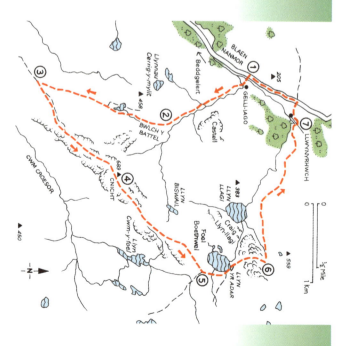

# Aberglasslyn Copper in the Hills

**4 miles (6.4km)** 2hrs 30min **Ascent:** 1,181ft (360m) ⚠

**Paths:** Well-maintained paths and tracks, 2 stiles

**Suggested map:** OS Explorer OL17 Snowdon

**Grid reference:** SH 597462

**Parking:** National Trust pay car park, Aberglaslyn

**Note:** Short section of riverside path in Aberglaslyn gorge is difficult and requires use of handholds

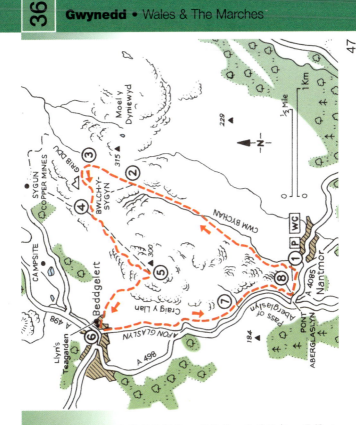

### A walk up to the old copper mines.

❶ Path starts to **L** of toilet block and goes under old railway bridge, before climbing through **Cwm Bychan**. After short climb path continues past iron pylons of aerial cableway.

❷ Beyond pylons, keep to **R** of cwm, ignoring paths forking **L**. Grassy corridor leads to col and stile in fence that is not shown on current maps. Turn **L** beyond stile and head for 3-way footpath signpost by rocks of **Grib Ddu**.

❸ Follow path on **L** ('To Beddgelert and Sygun') and go over another ladder stile. After veering **L**, around small rocky knoll, path winds steeply down hillside to cairn at **Bwlch-y-Sygyn**. Here you'll see a shallow peaty pool in green hollow to **L**.

❹ Path now heads southwest along mountain's northwestern 'edge', overlooking **Beddgelert**. Take **L** fork to pass signpost; follow 'Beddgelert' direction.

❺ Watch out for large cairn, highlighting turn-off **R** for **Beddgelert**. Clear stony path weaves through rhododendron and rock, goes through kissing gate in wall half-way down, then descends further to edge of **Beddgelert**, where little lane passing cottage of Penlan leads to **Afon Glaslyn**.

❻ Turn **L** to follow river for short way. Don't cross footbridge over river but turn **L** through kissing gate to follow Glaslyn's east bank. The path joins and follows trackbed of old Welsh Highland Railway.

❼ Just before 1st tunnel, descend **R** to follow rough path down to river. Handholds screwed into rocks allow passage on difficult but short section. Path continues through riverside woodland and over boulders to **Pont Aberglaslyn**.

❽ Here, turn **L** up steps and follow dirt path through woods. After crossing railway trackbed turn **R**, then **R** again to go under old railway bridge back to car park.

# Roman Steps With the Drovers

**7 miles (11.3km)** 4hrs **Ascent:** 1,575ft (480m) ▲

**Paths:** Peaty paths through heather and farm tracks, 11 stiles

**Suggested map:** OS Explorer OL18 Harlech, Porthmadog & Bala

**Grid reference:** SH 646314

**Parking:** Llyn Cwm Bychan

**Along one of Snowdonia's oldest highways.**

**1** Go through gate at back of car park at **Llyn Cwm Bychan**, and over paved causeway across stream. Beyond stile path climbs up through woodland.

**2** Over stile leave woodland behind and cross stream on small bridge. Path nicks **R** to go through gap in wall, then **L** again, heading towards Rhinog rocks. It slowly veers **L** and, now slabbed with 'steps', climbs through heather-clad rocky ravine to enter nature reserve. Steps continue to climb to cairn marking highest point along rocky pass of **Bwlch Tyddiad**.

**3** Over col, continue along path which descends into grassy moorland basin beneath **Rhinog Fawr** then, beyond a stile, enter conifers of **Coed y Brenin** plantation. Well-defined footpath tucks away under trees and eventually comes to wide flinted forestry road, along which you turn **L**.

**4** After about 1 mile (1.6km) road swings **R** to head east, watch out for waymarked path on **L** that will

eventually take you out of forest. After a short way along this path, waymark guides route **L**, then another to **R** to pass ruins of **Hafod-Gynfal**. Beyond this head north to go over ladder stile and out of forest.

**5** There's no path across grassy moor of **Moel y Gwartheg**. Just head north here, with cliffs of **Craig Wion** well to your **L** and bridge across huge expanse of Llyn Trawsfynydd at 5 minutes past hour.

**6** Further downhill footpath ends on **L**-**H** side guides you down towards isolated cottage of **Wern Fach**. Cross over stile just short of cottage, then turn **L** uphill, following clear waymarks which will guide you over 1st of many ladder stiles.

**7** Wet moorland footpath climbs up to lonely col of **Bwlch Gwylim**, narrow pass between **Clip** and **Craig Wion**. Here **Cwm Bychan** and start of walk come back into view. Footpath now descends to southwest, through heather, before turning **R** to head down slopes back to car park.

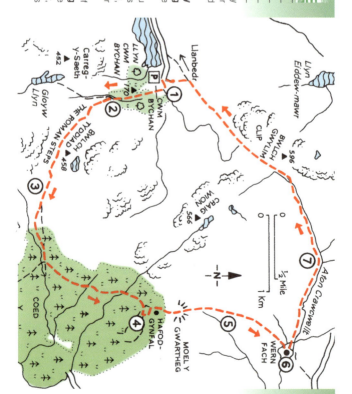

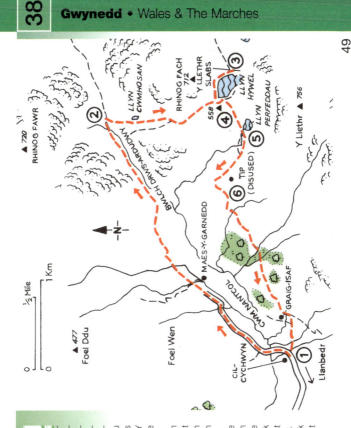

# Nantcol High Lakes and Highwaymen

**5½ miles (8.8km)** 3hrs 30min **Ascent:** 1,378ft (420m) ▲ ②

**Paths:** Peaty paths through heather and farm tracks, 1 stile

**Suggested map:** OS Explorer OL18 Harlech, Porthmadog & Bala

**Grid reference:** SH 633259

**Parking:** Small fee for parking at Cil-cychwyn farm

### Wild Nantcol and a lake between two peaks.

**①** From farm at **Cil-cychwyn**, follow narrow lane, which bends **L** to cross Afon Cwmnantcol at Pont Cerrig (bridge) before resuming its course up valley. At road's terminus near **Maes-y-garnedd** farm, continue climb on wallside path through upper Nantcol. It traverses lower south flanks of **Rhinog Fawr** before entering dark pass of **Bwlch Drws-Ardudwy**. This was a drovers' route along which cattle would have been driven to markets in the Marches and the Midlands, and consequently the haunt of highwaymen.

**②** On reaching marshy basin beneath **Rhinog Fawr** and **Rhinog Fach** go over ladder stile in wall on **R**. Follow narrow path climbing through heather and passing west shores of **Llyn Cwmhosan**, and beneath boulder and screes of Rhinog Fach's west face. Beyond this, route comes to shores of **Llyn Hywel**.

**③** For best views follow path, bouldery in places, around north and east sides of tarn to reach top of huge **Y Llethr Slabs**, that plummet into lake. You could do a complete circuit of Llyn Hywel, but this would mean climbing much higher up the slopes of Y Llethr. It is much easier to retrace your steps to the lake's outlet point, then continue along west shores.

**④** Turn **R** to follow sketchy narrow path down to Llyn **Perfeddau** which is visible from top. Intermittent peat path descends through heather, which is mixed with tussocky grass little further down, to reach north shores of lake.

**⑤** Follow wall running behind lake then, after ½ mile (800m), go through gap in wall to follow grassy path that rounds rocky knoll high above **Nantcol** before passing old mine. Here path becomes prominent track that winds past mine workings before veering **L** (west southwest) to descend gradually into Nantcol's valley.

**⑥** Through woodland and high pasture, track passes **Graig-Isaf** farm before reaching valley road at Cil-cychwyn.

# Barmouth The Sublime Mawddach

**6 miles (9.7km)** 4hrs **Ascent:** 656ft (200m) ▲

**Paths:** A bridge, good tracks and woodland paths, 5 stiles

**Suggested map:** OS Explorer OL23 Cadair Idris & Llyn Tegid

**Grid reference:** SH 613155

**Parking:** Car park on seafront

Follow in the illustrious footsteps of Wordsworth, Darwin and Ruskin on this lovely watery walk.

**❶** Follow promenade round **harbour**, then go over footbridge across estuary (toll). On reaching path along south shore of estuary, turn **L** to follow grassy embankment that leads to track rounding wooded knoll of **Fegla Fawr**.

**❷** When it comes to terraced houses of **Mawddach Crescent**, follow track that passes to rear of houses. Ignore tarmac lane going **R**, but continue along shoreline until you reach gate on **R** marking start of a good path heading across marshes of Arthog.

**❸** Turn **L** along old railway track, then leave it just before crossing of little Arthog Estuary and turn **R** along tarmac lane that passes small car park. Turn **L** over ladder stile and follow raised embankment to wall, which now leads path to main Dolgellau road next to **St Catherine's Church**.

**❹** Turn **L** along road past church, then cross road for footpath beginning with some steps into woodland. A good waymarked path now climbs by **Arthog**. Here you are presented with an elevated view of all that you have seen so far, the estuary, the sandbars, the mountains and the yawning bridge. This is the landscape that inspired artists like JMW Turner and Richard Wilson who came to capture the beauty and changing light of the area.

**❺** Beyond stile at top of woods, turn **R** to reach lane. Turn **R** along descending lane, then **L** along stony track passing cottage of Merddyn. Path leaves track on **L** and descends into more woodland, beneath boulders of old quarry and down to Dolgellau road by Arthog Village Hall.

**❻** Turn **R** along road, then **L** along path back to railway track and Mawddach Trail. Turn **L** along trail and follow it past **Morfa Mawddach Station** and back across **Barmouth's** bridge.

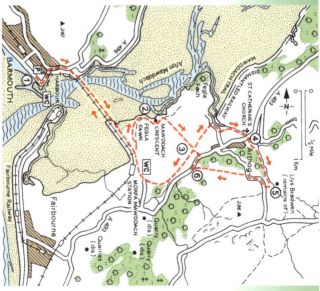

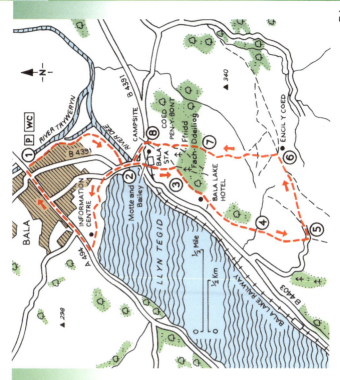

# Bala A View of Bala's Lake

**5 miles (8km)** 3hrs **Ascent:** 656ft (200m)

**Paths:** Woodland and field paths, 8 stiles

**Suggested map:** OS Explorer OL23 Cadair Idris & Llyn Tegid

**Grid reference:** SH 929361 **Parking:** Car park at entrance to Bala town from east

## The best view of Wales' largest natural lake.

**1** Go to northeast side of car park in **Bala** to access riverside path, where you turn **R** to follow raised embankment along west bank of **Tryweryn**. After dog-leg to **R**, which passes through 2 kissing gates, footpath continues, first by banks of **Tryweryn**, then by north banks of **Dee**.

**2** At road by Bala's lake, **Llyn Tegid**, turn L then **R** along Llangower road. Go through kissing gate to cross small field to **Bala Station** on **Bala Lake Railway**. Footbridge allows you to cross track before traversing 2 small fields.

**3** Turn **R** along cart track, and pass behind **Bala Lake Hotel**. Waymarker points direction up grassy bank on **L**, and path continues southwest, accompanied by fence on R.

**4** After crossing stream, next to little cottage on R-H side, route comes upon area of rough pastureland interspersed with outcrops of rock, rushes and bracken. Here footpath on ground all but disappears.

Ascend half **L** (roughly southwards) to reach fenceline at top, then aim for ladder stile in middle distance.

**5** Turn **L** along tarred lane just before that ladder stile. Where road ends take **R** fork track that ploughs through recently felled conifer plantation.

**6** At whitewashed house of **Encil y Coed**, turn **L** off track to climb **L-H** of 2 ladder stiles, then follow grooved grass track heading north across high pastures. Where track bends to R leave it to descend steeply to another ladder stile. Well-waymarked path continues north, with **Bala** town ahead.

**7** Go over partially hidden step stile into commercial forestry plantations of **Coed Pen-y-Bont**. Narrow footpath descends to bottom edge of woods (ignore forestry track you meet on way down).

**8** At bottom of woods turn **R** along track to road by **Pen-y-Bont Campsite**. Turn L along road, walking back towards town, then turn **L** again to follow lakeside footpath past **information centre**. At main road, turn **R** to explore town centre.

# The Dysynni Valley Castell y Bere

**5 miles (8km)** 3hrs **Ascent:** 656ft (200m) ▲2

**Paths:** Field paths and tracks, 16 stiles

**Suggested map:** OS Explorer OL23 Cadair Idris & Llyn Tegid

**Grid reference:** SH 677069

**Parking:** Car park in Pandy Square, Abergynolwyn village centre

## Exploring the valleys where the Welsh princes held out against the might of Edward I.

**1** Cross road to **Railway Inn** and take lane ('Llanfihangel'). At far side of bridge over **Dysynni river**, turn **R** through kissing gate and trace north banks. Beyond 2nd step stile, path turns **L** before climbing steps beside tall leylandii to reach lane.

**2** Turn **R** along lane which bears east through Dysynni Valley and beneath woodlands of **Coed Meriafel**. At junction with **B4405** turn **L**, over stile and climb northwest across field. Continue over 2 more stiles to woodland path. Climb along this to reach forestry track near top edge of woods.

**3** Turn **L** along track which climbs out of woods before veering **R** to gate and stile. Over stile, follow wall on **L**. Ignore faint grass track that goes ahead and across field. The route stays low and veers **L** through high grassy cwm with stream developing on **L**.

**4** After traversing several fields, path joins flinted

track but leaves it after 200yds (183m) for streamside path on **L**. This descends into woods and stays close to stream. After passing several cascades it comes out of woods to reach track leading to road at **Llanfihangel-y-pennant** just opposite **chapel**.

**5** Turn **L** past chapel and **Castell y Bere** (detour through gates on **R** for closer look). Just beyond castle, take path on **L** that climbs to gate at top **R-H** corner of field. Beyond gate turn **R** along farm track passing **Caerberllan** farm to road. Turn **R** along road, **L** at crossroads and cross **Pont Ystumanner** (bridge).

**6** On other side, footpath signpost highlights track on **L** to pass **Rhiwlas farm** then continues as green path high above river. Path crosses slopes of **Gamallt** and swings gradually **L** with valley.

**7** Beyond river gorge, path approaches back of **Abergynolwyn** village and turns **L** to cross old iron bridge across river. Beyond it, turn **R** along unsurfaced street to return to village centre.

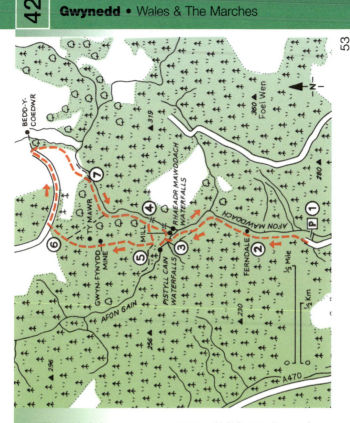

# Dolgellau The King's Forest

**4 miles (6.4km)** 2hrs **Ascent:** 660ft (200m)

**Paths:** Forest tracks and paths, 2 stiles

**Suggested map:** OS Explorer OL18 Harlech, Porthmadog & Bala

**Grid reference:** SH 735263

**Parking:** Tyddyn Gwladys forest Car Park near Ganllwyd

**Two waterfalls, hidden deep in the forest.**

1 Turn **R** out of car park and follow flinted forestry track with **Afon Mawddach** below R. Track passes beneath terraced Mostyn cottages.

2 Take higher track to **L** of **Ferndale** holiday cottages – once gold mine workshops and blasting plant. Gold has been mined throughout Wales for centuries, but there were large finds of good quality gold in the 19th century, when Dolgellau became another Klondyke. Track eventually swings **R** to cross **Afon Gain**, close to its confluence with **Mawddach**.

3 On reaching other side, detour **L** along rough path to take a closer look at **Pistyll Cain waterfalls**. The impressive cascades splash 150ft (45m) against dark rocks into a deep pool below. Return to main track, and turn **L** to old mine's **mill** buildings.

4 Just beyond mill are **Rhaeadr Mawddach falls**. Ignore footbridges here and double back **L** on slaty path climbing through conifer plantation – ignore

cycle route on R, near beginning of this path.

5 After winding up hillside, path comes to junction. Ignore signed footpath going straight ahead, but turn **R** on track with white-topped post (no 30). This soon becomes grassy path that comes out of forest at small gate, and continues as enclosed track through high pastures in area that was once main **Gwynfynydd Mine**. Track passes above **Ty Mawr** farm, and becomes tarred lane.

6 Turn **R** on meeting country lane and follow it almost to **Bedd y Coedwr** farm. Footpath signpost points way downhill on field path that stays to R of some attractive birchwoods. Path veers **R** through heather-cloaked scrub and becomes rough and overgrown in places until it reaches old mine track by banks of Mawddach.

7 Follow track past shafts of gold mines to reach outward route by **Rhaeadr Mawddach**. Retrace your steps to car park.

# Talsarnau The Tecwyn Lakes

**5 miles (8km)** 3hrs **Ascent:** 800ft (244m) ▲

**Paths:** Well-defined paths, lanes, 9 stiles
**Suggested map:** OS Outdoor Leisure 18 Harlech, Portmadog & Bala
**Grid reference:** SH 612360
**Parking:** Car park just off main road at Talsarnau

**Unknown lakes and the breezy salt marshes.**

❶ Turn **R** out of car park, then cross road. Climb lane opposite, then take **L** 'Llandecwyn' fork. Lane climbs hillsides and beneath **Coed Garth-byr** (woods).

❷ After about ¾ mile (1200m) go through small gate on signposted path that climbs hillside pasture with fence to L. Go through gate at top, into oakwoods. Through 3rd gate path descends to country lane.

❸ Across lane follow signposted track towards **Garth-byr** farm. Don't enter farm complex but turn **L** along grass path. Take higher **L** fork path 200yds (182m) beyond farmhouse, then take **R** of 2 gates. Path heads northeast through scrub. Crumbled wall joins from L and path follows it via thicker woodland. You can see **Llyn Tecwyn Isaf** through trees.

❹ Go over stile in wall and follow path to lane. Turn **L** along lane, round north shores of Llyn Tecwyn Isaf, then take lane on **R**, which climbs to Llandecwyn **church**, where tarmac ends.

❺ Continue along stony track, and go through gate to reach west shores of **Llyn Tecwyn uchaf**.

❻ Turn **L** along gated track that descends beneath pylons through narrow rocky valley. On nearing main road at bottom ignore grassy track to R, but climb ahead on grass path which passes R of outbuilding and L of cottage to reach lane in **Llandecwyn**.

❼ Turn **R** along this, cross main road and follow lane towards railway station. Turn **L** along lane with footpath sign, then climb ladder stile in front of **Bryn Glas** (cottage) and skirt base of rocky knoll beyond. Climb ladder stile, and cross railway (take care).

❽ Over another stile path follows flood embankment on edge of coastal marshes of **Glastraeth**. Across the wide estuary you can see Portmeirion and the mountains of Snowdonia, including Snowdon itself.

❾ Leave embankment on reaching stony track, which heads directly for houses of **Talsarnau**. Again cross railway with care and follow lane back to village.

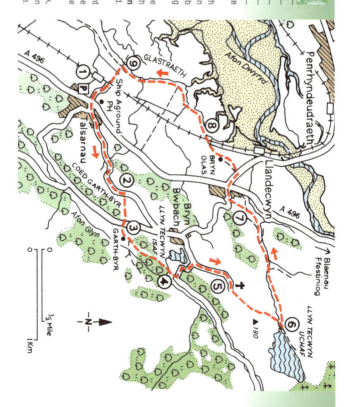

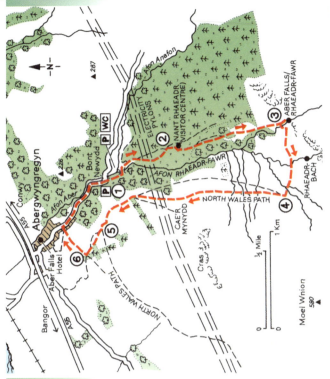

# Abergwyngregyn Twin Falls

**5 miles (8km)** 3hrs **Ascent:** 820ft (250m) ⛰

**Paths:** Well-defined paths and farm tracks; 9 stiles

**Suggested map:** OS Explorer OL17 Snowdon

**Grid reference:** SH 783774

**Parking:** Small car park at entrance to glen. Large pay car park over bridge beyond

### A fine mountain glen with two waterfalls

**1** Go through gate at south end of lower car park, and follow path through woods surrounding **Afon Rhaeadr**. Cross river on footbridge, go through gate at other side, and turn **R** to follow wide track heading south through pastures of valley.

**2** After passing under rows of pylons you reach visitor centre, which is housed in old farmstead of Nant Rhaeadr (marked Nant on maps). The glen is now part of the Coedydd Aber National Nature Reserve, which was set up in 1975 by the Nature Conservancy Council (now English Nature) as an example of a broad-leaved woodland habitat. The visitor centre explains the workings of the valley, past and present. Beyond Nant Rhaeadr path climbs steadily through valley with the top of the **Aber Falls** visible ahead.

**3** Path climbs stone steps on last knoll before base of falls. Here continuing path turns **R**, over ladder stile, but first you will want to get nearer to falls. Short

detour descends into wooded hollow. Here the thunderous falls plummet hundreds of feet down cliffs of quartz-streaked Cambrian granophyre. Scrub birch trees eke out an existence high on the rock-ledges, as do liverworts, rare mosses and lichens, primroses and anemones. Return to ladder stile. On other side follow path marked 'North Wales Path only; no short return to Aber', which heads west beneath cliffs to pass beneath Rhaeadr Bach. (falls).

**4** Path swings N along western valley slopes and becomes track on slopes of Cae'r Mynydd. After rounding strip of conifer woods and passing sheep pens track veers **L**.

**5** Just before entering another conifer plantation turn **R** at junction of tracks to descend northwest towards northern tip of those same woods.

**6** Turn **R** on waymarked narrow path descending northeast down to Abergwyngregyn. On reaching lane turn **R** for short riverside walk to car park.

# Holyhead Mountain Last Stop Before Ireland

**4½ miles (7.2km)** 2hrs 30min **Ascent:** 886ft (270m) ▲

**Paths:** Well-maintained paths and tracks. Heathland, coastal cliffs and rocky hills

**Suggested map:** OS Explorer 262 Anglesey West

**Grid reference:** SH 210818

**Parking:** RSPB car park

Rugged and rocky Holy Island offers some of the best **walking in Anglesey.**

**1** Take path signed for RSPB centre, past **Ellin's Tower,** small castellated building, then climb along path back to road which should be followed to its end.

**2** If you're not visiting **South Stack Lighthouse,** climb **R** on path passing concrete shelter. The path detours **R** to round BT aerials and dishes. At crossroads go **L,** heading back to coast, then take **L** fork. Ignore next **L,** dead end path. The footpath required works its way over north shoulder of **Holyhead Mountain.**

**3** Ignore paths to summit, but keep **L** on good path heading north towards **North Stack.**

**4** After passing through grassy walled enclosure path descends in zig-zags down some steep slopes before coming to rocky platform, where **Fog Signal Station** and island of **North Stack** come into full view. Retrace your steps back up zig-zags and towards

**Holyhead Mountain.**

**5** With summit path in sight, take a narrow path heading sharp **L** across heath. This joins another narrow path contouring round east side of mountain. Turn **R** along it, later ignoring another summit path coming in from **L.** Beyond mountain, take a **R** fork as path comes to a wall. Follow path downhill towards rough pastureland.

**6** Go down grassy walled track before turning **R** along another, similar one. This soon becomes rough path traversing more heathland, now to south of **Holyhead Mountain.**

**7** Near to **quarry** with lake, take path veering **R** alongside rocks of **Holyhead Mountain.** The BT aerials and dishes can be seen again on horizon by now. Follow paths towards them then, at crossroads, turn **L** and **L** again, along a concrete footpath leading back to road.

**8** Turn **L** along road to car park.

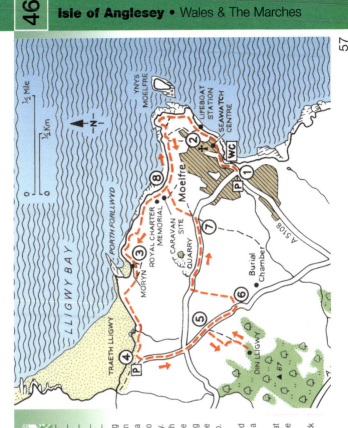

# Moelfre The Ancient Village

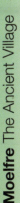

**3 miles (4.8km)** 1hr 30min **Ascent:** Negligible

**Paths:** Well-defined coastal and field paths, 4 stiles

**Suggested map:** OS Explorer 263 Anglesey East

**Grid reference:** SH 511862

**Parking:** Car park at entrance to village

Walk along Anglesey's beautiful east coast to discover a remarkably intact ancient village.

**1** From car park, follow main road down to shore. Here, where road swings **L** and uphill for village centre, leave it for shoreline path on **R**.

**2** Pass **Seawatch Centre** and **lifeboat station** and ignore footpath signs pointing inland. Instead follow a clear coast path that looks across to island of **Ynys Moelfre**. After passing to **R** of some terraced cottages and going through couple of kissing gates, path crosses **caravan site**. It then goes through another kissing gate and climbs past **Royal Charter memorial** to those who died when the British cutter was dashed on the rocks in a storm in 1859.

**3** After swinging **L** into **Porth Forllwyd**, go through gate and then through a narrow ginnel that rounds bay, past cottage of **Moryn** into bay of **Traeth Lligwy**.

**4** On reaching beach car park, turn **L** along narrow lane before going straight ahead at next crossroads.

**5** Take next path on **R** ('Din Lligwy'). Before visiting village you turn half **R** across field to old chapel, then half **L** towards woods, where you'll find **Din Lligwy**, a wonderfully preserved Celtic settlement dating back to the last years of the Roman Empire in the 4th century. Enter the foundations through thick rubble walls which would have been added as protection against the Romans. The circular huts inside were the living quarters, while the large rectangular hut you can see in the top R-H corner was the smelting workshop. Return to lane and turn **R** along it.

**6** After 275yds (251m), turn **L** along a signed footpath which, after an initial dog-leg to R, follows a field edge to roadside **quarry** at Aberstrecht.

**7** Turn **R** along lane, then **L** along a farm lane at Caeau-gleision. This brings you back to shoreline **caravan site** met earlier in walk.

**8** Turn **R** beyond it and follow shoreline path back to start.

# Capel Curig An Alpine Journey

**Paths:** Generally clear and surfaced, 9 stiles

**Suggested map:** OS Explorer OL17 Snowdon

**Grid reference:** SJ 720582

**Parking:** Behind Joe Brown's shop at Capel Curig

**4 miles (6.4km)** 2hrs **Ascent:** 295ft (90m) (doesn't include pinnacle scramble) ▲

Discovering the valley where the rocks and mountains provide challenging ground for today's climbers and mountaineers.

**❶** The path begins at ladder stile by war memorial on A5 and climbs towards **Y Pincin** – large craggy outcrop cloaked in wood and bracken. Go over another stile and keep to north of outcrop. Those who want to go to top should do so from the northeast, where gradients are easier. It's fun, but take care! You'll need to retrace your steps.

**❷** Continue east across woods and marshy ground, keeping to south of great crags of **Clogwyn Mawr**. On reaching couple of ladder stiles, ignore path back down to road, but maintain your direction across hillside.

**❸** Just beyond footbridge over **Nant y Geuallt**, leave main footpath and follow less well-defined path across marshy ground. This veers southeast to cross another stream before coming to prominent track.

**❹** Turn **R** along track, but leave it beyond ladder stile and at 4-way meeting of paths. Go **L** here and follow path down into some woods. Take **R-H** fork descending to road near **Ty'n y Coed Inn.**

**❺** Turn **L** down road, then **R**, along lane over **Pont-Cyfyng.** Go **R** again beyond bridge to follow footpath that traces **Llugwy** to another bridge opposite Cobdens Hotel. Don't cross this time, but scramble **L** over some rocks before continuing through woods of **Coed Bryn-engan,** where path soon becomes wide track.

**❻** After passing cottage of **Bryn-engan,** track comes to bridge at head of **Mymbyr** lakes. Turn **R** across it, then **L** along road for short way.

**❼** Go over next ladder stile on **R-H** side of road and take higher of 2 tracks swinging round to **R.** This hugs foot of southern Glyder slopes.

**❽** When you get beyond **Gelli** farm turn **R** to follow cart track back to car park.

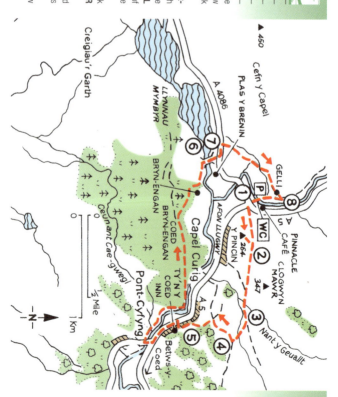

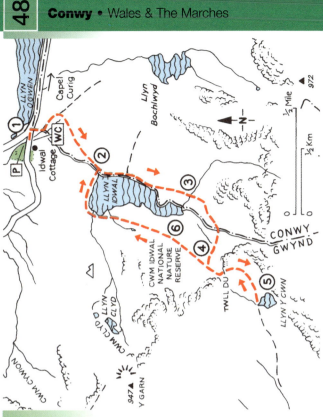

# Ogwen The Devil's Kitchen

**3 miles (4.8km)** 2hrs 30min **Ascent:** 1,706ft (520m) ▲▲

**Paths:** Well-defined paths, 2 stiles

**Suggested map:** OS Explorer OL17 Snowdon

**Grid reference:** SH 649603

**Parking:** Small car park at Ogwen

**Explore the most perfect hanging valley in Snowdonia – its rock ledges and Hanging Gardens.**

❶ The Cwm Idwal nature trail starts to **L** of toilet block at Ogwen and climbs up hillside to pass some impressive waterfalls before turning **R** and continuing up hill.

❷ Go through a gate in a fence, which marks boundary of **National Nature Reserve**, and turn **L** along side of **Llyn Idwal's** eastern shores. The clear footpath climbs into dark shadows of Cwm Idwal.

❸ Now leave nature trail, which turns R to complete circuit around lake. Instead ascend beneath rock-climbing grounds of Idwal Slabs and across stream of Nant Ffan, beyond which footpath zig-zags up rough boulder ground to foot of **Twll Du** – Devil's Kitchen. If weather, and preferably forecast too, are fine, climb to **Llyn y Cwn** at top of this impressive defile; if not, skip this bit and turn **R** to Point ❻. The rich soils on the

crags around Twll Du allow many species of Arctic plants to flourish free from animal grazing. Collectively the foliage seems to flow down the rocks and you can see why it is called the Hanging Gardens.

❹ To ascend Twll Du climb engineered path as it angles **L** up rock face, which will now be on your R-H side, above an extensive area of scree and boulder. At top you come to a relatively gentle (by comparison) grassy hollow between rising summits of **Y Garn**, to R, and **Glyder Fawr**, to L.

❺ Just beyond first grassy mounds you come across small tarn of Llyn y Cwn, which makes a great picnic spot. Now retrace your steps carefully to bottom of **Twll Du.**

❻ From here descend rocky ground down to western side of **Llyn Idwal**. The path reaches, then rounds, northern shoreline to meet outward route at gate near outflow stream, Point ❷. Now follow route of your outward journey back to car park at **Ogwen.**

# Llyn Crafnant The Twin Lakes

**5 miles** (8km) 3hrs **Ascent:** 656ft (200m) ▲▲

**Paths:** Clear paths and forestry tracks, 7 stiles

**Suggested map:** OS Explorer OL17 Snowdon

**Grid reference:** SH 756618

**Parking:** Forestry car park, north of Llyn Crafnant

**Discover two lakes, one to inspire poets present and one that inspired bards past.**

**1** Turn R out of car park and follow lane to north end of **Llyn Crafnant**, a lake surrounded by woodland, pasture and hills. Turn R and follow forestry track along northwest shores of lake.

**2** Ignore 1st stile on **L**, and instead climb with forestry track. Keep watch for waymarked footpath on which you should descend **L** to pass beneath cottage of **Hendre**. Go over footbridge on **R**, then turn **L** down track past modern chalets.

**3** Turn **L** along road which heads back towards lake. Leave this at **telephone box** for path ('Llyn Geirionydd') and waymarked with blue-capped posts. This climbs through conifer forests and over shoulder of **Mynydd Deulyn**.

**4** Descend on winding forestry track, still following obvious blue-capped posts. Ignore track forking to R – that leads to Llyn Bychan.

**5** On reaching valley floor, leave track to go over step stile on **L**. The path crosses a field beneath **Ty-newydd** cottage before tracing **Llyn Geirionydd's** shoreline. At northern end of lake, path keeps to **R** of a wall and meets farm track.

**6** Turn **L** along this, then **R** to **Taliesin Monument** erected in 1850 to commemorate the 6th-century bard who is known to have lived here at the northern end of Geirionydd. Many of Taliesin's poems recall tales of magic and mystery, and many of them relate to the heroics of King Arthur, who some believe was his one-time master. Descend to green path heading northwest, then north, descending towards Crafnant Valley.

**7** Veer **L** to cross ladder stile and follow undulating path over rock and heather knolls.

**8** Path eventually swings **L** to reach old **mine**. Here, take lower track on **R** which descends back to valley road and forest car park.

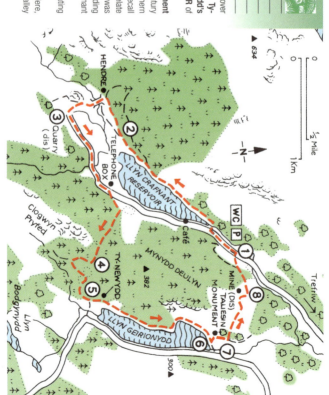

# Dolgarrog Tragic Disaster Area

**7 miles (11.3km)** 3hrs 30min **Ascent:** 328ft (100m)

**Paths:** Tracks and country lanes, 4 stiles

**Suggested map:** OS Explorer OL17 Snowdon

**Grid reference:** SH 731663

**Parking:** Car park at the end of road

**Discovering grim secrets, high in one of the Carneddau's loneliest valleys.**

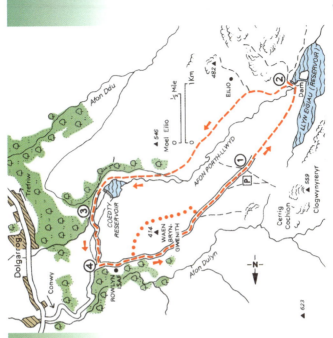

**①** Follow track heading roughly southwest from car park into jaws of **Eigiau**. This track turns L below main dam and goes over a bridge across reservoir's outflow stream. One November night in 1925 the Eigiau dam disintegrated and the waters came thundering into the upper valley of the Afon Porth-Llwyd towards the Coedty Reservoir. That dam also broke, the waters carrying huge boulders down towards the hapless village of Dolgarrog, which was devastated and 16 lives were lost. It is said that the death toll would have been higher were it not for the fact that many of the villagers were at the cinema, which was situated on higher ground. The dam was never rebuilt.

**②** Turn **L** along greener track that traces river's southeast banks, ignoring path on R beneath **Eilio**. The gated track passes **Coedty Reservoir** and leads to a country lane by dam. From the **reservoir** you can

see the boulders, by the oak-shaded river banks, deposited there on that fateful night.

**③** Follow lane as it descends to cross river, then climbs out on to hillside high above Conwy Valley.

**④** Turn **L** at T-junction to pass **Rowlyn Isaf** farm on your R. The quickest and recommended route follows this quiet country lane back to car park.

**An Alternative Route**

It is possible to get back by using path south of **Waen Bryn-gwenith**. However it's very rough in early stages where path is lost in thick bracken. For purist however a signposted path from woods, Point A, beyond farm climbs beside a wall and fades near top end of woods. Here look out for small gate on **L**, Point B. Now you have to fight through thick bracken to go through to next field where you turn **R** to get to open hillside, Point C. Stay above wall/fence. As path nears road go over ladder stile in fence then turn **R** to another one at roadside. Turn **L** along road to get back to car park.

# Conwy Castle Stronghold

**6½ miles (10.4km)** 4hrs **Ascent:** 1,214ft (370m) ⚠

**Paths:** Good paths and easy-to-follow moorland tracks, 6 stiles

**Suggested map:** OS Explorer OL17 Snowdon

**Grid reference:** SH 782776

**Parking:** Large car park on Llanrwst Road behind Conwy Castle

**Conwy's castle and a remote Celtic fort.**

❶ From Conwy Quay head northwest along waterfront, past Smallest House and under town walls. Fork **R** along tarmac waterside footpath that rounds **Bodlondeb Wood.** Turn **L** along road, past school and on to **A547.** Cross road, then railway line by footbridge. Lane beyond skirts wood to another lane where you turn **R.**

❷ Another waymarker guides you on to a footpath on **R** that, beyond stile, ascends wooded hillsides to **Conwy Mountain.** Follow undulating crest of Conwy Mountain past **Castell Caer.**

❸ Several tracks converge in fields of **Pen-pyra.** Here, follow signposts for **North Wales** Path along track heading southwest over L shoulder of **Alltwen** and down to metalled road traversing **Sychnant Pass.**

❹ Follow footpath from other side of road, skirting woods on your L. Pass **Gwern Engen** on your L-H side and continue to pass to L of **Lodge,** to reach a lane

and continue to pass to L of **Lodge**, to reach a lane

junction, into **Groesffordd** village. Cross road, then take road ahead that swings to **R** past a telephone box, then L (southeast) towards **Plas Iolyn.**

❺ Turn **L** at next junction, then **R** at signposted enclosed footpath crossing fields to **B5106.** Turn **L** along road, then **R** at entrance to **caravan park,** following frequent waymarkers through scrubland and over several stiles. After crossing surfaced vehicle track, and descending into little hollow, path climbs **L** (north) along pastured ridge, with telephone mast ahead.

❻ Turn **L** at road then go **R** to pass to R-H side of telephone mast and **Bryn-locyn** farm. At **Coed Benarth** wood, turn **L** then follow narrow path northwards through woods.

❼ Cross ladder stile on **L-H** side and descend field to roadside gate at bottom. Turn **R** on to **B5106** to return to quayside, or turn **L** to return to main car park.

Turn **R** along lane then turn **L,** when you reach next

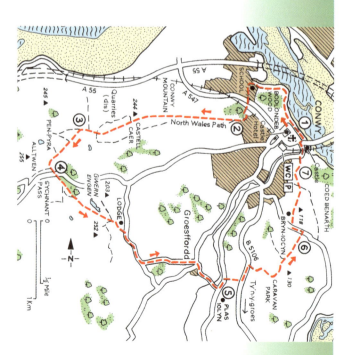

# Tal y Fan Stones and Settlements

**5 miles (8km)** 3hrs **Ascent: 984ft (300m)** ▲

**Paths:** Cart tracks and narrow mountain paths, 7 stiles

**Suggested map:** OS Explorer 0L17 Snowdon

**Grid reference:** SH 720715

**Parking:** Car park at end of Bwlch y Ddeufaen road, off B5106 Conwy–Llanrwst road

**Visit the most northerly 2,000ft (610m) hill in Wales and see what remains from ancient settlers.**

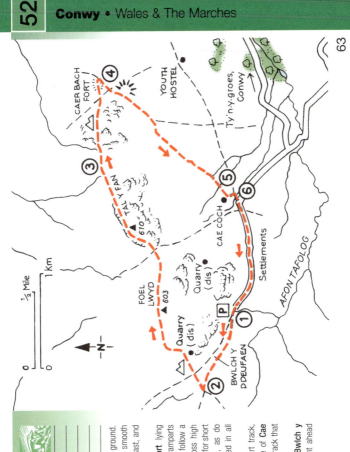

① From car park at top of metalled section of road to **Bwlch y Ddeufaen**, continue along road, which is now unsurfaced, and follow it past ancient standing stones to high pass itself, where you go through a gate in crossing wall.

② Turn **R** and follow course of wall, which traverses pass, goes under 3 lines of electricity pylons, and climbs steep rocky slopes of **Foel Lwyd**. A narrow footpath continues, first descending to a little saddle, or col, then climbing to even rockier summit of **Tal y Fan**. You should be able to pick out the field systems of the Bronze-Age farmers below the road in the valley of the Tafolog and in the pastures to the north of the youth hostel.

③ The descending footpath still follows line of dry-stone wall, but it stays with more even ground on L–H side. The wall turns R by particularly steep ground. Here you leave it to follow a pathless but smooth grassy ride, aiming for **Caer Bach fort**, to east, and prominent rocky knoll beyond.

④ Reach the remains of **Caer Bach fort** lying beneath the turf and gorse, but with its earth ramparts and a circle of stones still visible. Turn **R** to follow a tumbled down wall heading southwest across high pastureland overlooking Conwy Valley. Except for short stretch this wall now acts as your guide, as do frequent ladder stiles and locked gates sited in all intervening cross-walls.

⑤ The footpath eventually becomes a cart track, which passes beneath whitewashed cottage of **Cae Coch** before turning **L** to join stony vehicle track that has come from **Rowen Youth Hostel**.

⑥ Turn **R** along track, which soon joins **Bwlch y Ddeufaen** road at sharp corner. Go straight ahead along road and follow it back to car park.

# 53 Nant-y-Coed Pass of the Two Stones

**5 miles (8km)** 3hrs **Ascent:** 1,214ft (370m) 2

**Paths:** Woodland, field and moorland paths, cart tracks, 5 stiles

**Suggested map:** OS Explorer OL17 Snowdon

**Grid reference:** SH 694739

**Parking:** Small car park on Newry Drive, Nant-y-Coed, Llanfairfechan

**A walk through one of the prettiest woods in Wales, to a high mountain pass.**

1 Go through gate beyond car park and follow stony path through woods of **Nant-y-Coed** and by north bank of stream. This valley, part of the Newry Estate, was a popular tourist attraction in the 1900s. Take more prominent **L** fork to pass pond, then cross stream using stepping stones. More stepping stones are used to cross a side stream before climbing to 2nd car park.

2 Follow signpost up valley and cross a footbridge over river to continue. Keep a sharp eye open for waymarks, which guide you along zig-zagging path in a complex series of criss-crossing tracks.

3 Path enters open moorland, starting as a grooved rush-filled track before deteriorating into sheep tracks through gorse fields. Aim for col between **Foel Lwyd** and **Drosgl**, to point where 3 lines of pylons straddle fells.

4 At **Bwlch y Ddeufaen** (pass of the two stones) faint path arcs **R**, to other side of col, where it joins **Roman road**. Turn **R** along track and follow it across rough moor.

5 On reaching crossroads of tracks, turn **R** ('**Llanfairfechan**'). You're now following waymarked course of North Wales Path over **Garreg Fawr**. After going over top of 1st grassy summit path veers **L** to rake down west side of hill, from where you can see the coastal sands and the Isle of Anglesey.

6 Take waymarked **R-H** fork rather than track following wall on L. This trends to **R**, goes through kissing gate in crossing wall, then descends to high pasture land overlooking **Nant-y-Coed**. Turn **L** down little enclosed ginnel that descends to road.

7 Turn **R** along road, which descends further to cross a bridge over Afon Llanfairfechan. At other side take narrow lane back to car park.

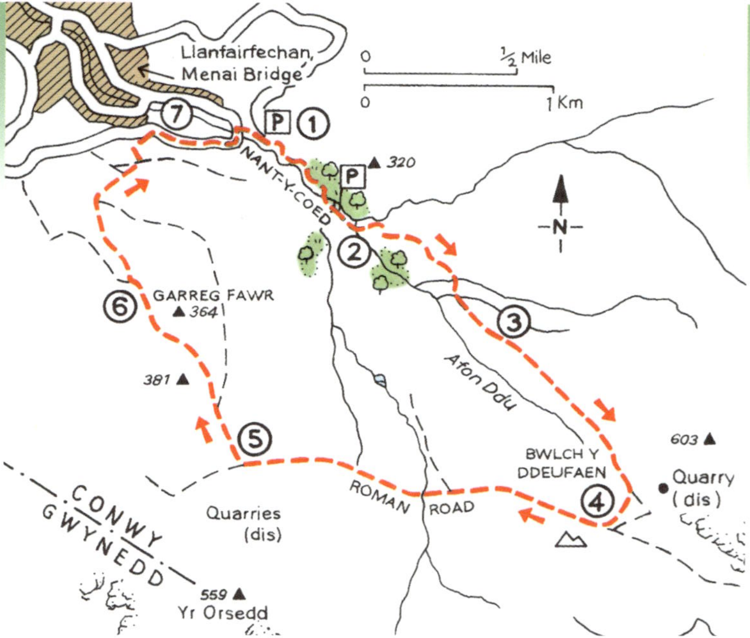

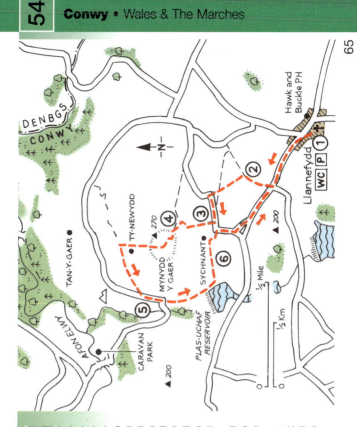

# Mynydd y Gaer With the Poet

**2½ miles (4km)** 1hr 30min **Ascent:** 886ft (270m)

**Paths:** Field paths and tracks, 2 stiles

**Suggested map:** OS Explorer 264 Vale of Clwyd

**Grid reference:** SH 981706

**Parking:** Llannefydd village car park

**Visit an Iron-Age fort and look down on the magnificent land- and seascapes that inspired the 19th-century Jesuit priest and poet Gerard Manley Hopkins.**

**1** Turn **L** out of car park and follow lane ('Llanfair TH', TH standing for Talhaiarn). Where road comes in from L, go though gate on **R-H** side and traverse fields with hedge and fence on your L.

**2** After going through 2nd gate turn **L** and follow hedge and fence, which is still on your L, uphill. Go through gate in small enclosure for caravan, turn **R**, then pass through another gate out on to metalled road. Turn **L** along road.

**3** Where road turns sharply to L, leave it and double-back to **R** on tarmac track climbing up to Bryn Hwyfa. Just past whitewashed cottage, turn **L** to walk along enclosed grass track climbing hill. Beyond gate grassy footpath winds through gorse and scrub before veering **L** beneath outer ring defences of Iron-Age fort.

**4** Where gorse bushes become more sparse, climb **R** to reach brow of hill. Go through farm gate to reach cairn which marks summit. Below and to the north you can see the **Afon Elwy** twisting and turning between low wooded hills. This is the landscape that inspired the 19th-century poet and Jesuit priest Gerard Manley Hopkins to write *In the Valley of the Elwy*. Descend north from here, to pick up track that passes a hilltop farm, **Ty-newydd**, before descending **L** to meet another lane.

**5** Turn **L** to walk along lane, but leave it at **R-H** bend for a lovely grass track continuing straight ahead to pass above shores of **Plas-uchaf Reservoir**. Once you are past lake, track swings **L** towards **Sychnant**.

**6** Beyond gate, follow track as it becomes path, winding through woodland before coming to lane that you left on outward route. Turn **R** along this lane and then take 1st **L**, continue straight ahead to return to **Llannefydd** village.

# Betws-y-Coed Llyn Elsi

4 miles (6.4km) 2hrs 30min **Ascent:** 840ft (256m)

**Paths:** Well-defined forest tracks and paths
**Suggested map:** OS Explorers OL17 Snowdon & OL18 Harlech, Porthmadog & Bala
**Grid reference:** SH 795565 (on Explorer OL17)
**Parking:** Car park by railway station

**A high lake with views to Snowdonian peaks.**

**❶** From car park go to main road, turn **L**, then **R** along road between **post office** and **church**. Road veers **R** behind church. Here, take 'Llyn Elsi' forestry track on **L**. This swings **L** and climbs through forest. It bends **R** to cross lively stream, then **L** again to resume steady climb through trees. Ignore narrow path on **R** (direct but steep path to lake).

**❷** Take **R** fork with one of many white waymarks (these will guide you to and around Llyn Elsi). Take **L** fork at next junction, then **R** as track climbs steadily through conifers.

**❸** Take **L** fork as the gradient eases to arrive at lakeshore. At various points around the lake you will be able to pick out many of the Snowdonian peaks. Moel Siabod is the nearest and most prominent, while others include the jagged crest of Glyder Fach, and Tryfan, whose ruffled top just peeps out from behind the Glyder ridge. Heather, birch and rowan add

variation to the dark backdrop of conifers surrounding the lake. In autumn their mottled rusty colours make this a very pleasing place to be.

**❹** Follow track **L** along lakeshore then leave it beyond south dam for a path climbing **R** into woods. This becomes a track that winds along west shore of lake.

**❺** Leave the track for path on **R** (still waymarked with white posts), which winds through scrub, then beneath north dam to arrive at the **monument** that was erected in 1914 to celebrate the enlargement of the lake.

**❻** With your back to memorial plaque take narrow path straight ahead (slightly **R** of one you just used). Follow this north to cross two forestry roads. Soon rooftops of **Betws y Coed** flicker through trees on **R**.

**❼** Path gradually veers **L**, descends beneath wooden electricity pylons down to join another forestry track taking route to A5 near Cross Foxes Hotel. Turn **R** along road, back into village.

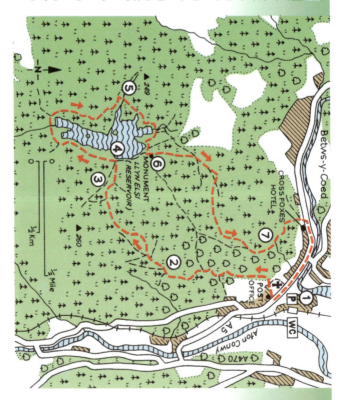

# Llandudno Alice's Wonderland

**5 miles (8km)** 2hrs 30min **Ascent:** 890ft (270m) ⛰

**Paths:** Well-defined paths and tracks

**Suggested map:** OS Explorer OL17 Snowdon

**Grid reference:** SH 783829 Snowdon

**Parking:** In any of the town car parks.

## The limestone sea-cliffs of Great Orme.

① It has been said that Lewis Carroll was inspired to write his *Alice's Adventures in Wonderland* after a visit to Llandudno, and seeing the caves, rabbit warrens and captivating scenery you can realise why. From Llandudno Pier walk along Marine Drive to Happy Valley Gardens and follow waymarks for Great Orme summit, along zig-zag surfaced path. At top of park go through gate and follow path into limestone ravine with dry-ski slope and toboggan run.

② Continue uphill and **R** to pass beneath limestone scars on to grassy slopes of **Great Orme**.

③ Further uphill and inland take middle of 3 paths signed 'summit'. Turn **R** at electric tramway's **Halfway Station**, following grassy path on nearside of track. After crossing St Tudno's road, climb along continuing path to summit. The **visitor centre** is open between Easter and October. Ex champion middleweight boxer Randolph Turpin used to be the landlord at the pub

next door, but tragically, after slipping into financial difficulties in 1966, he shot himself.

④ Go round north side of summit pub and follow waymarked path descending grassy hillside in direction of **St Tudno's church** and graveyard. Turn **L** along stony track near to its junction with tarmac road, and follow it round field-edges of **Parc Farm**.

⑤ Past rocks of **Free Trade Loaf**, path turns **L**, still following field-edge. Turn **L** again at cairn. You have now rounded Great Orme on to south side. It's worth detouring from wall to see cliff-edge and view across to Conwy Bay and Carneddau Mountains.

⑥ When cliff path runs out, return to wall and follow track, now high above cliffs. Ignore well-used path going **L** for summit complex, but instead take path bearing half **L**. Turn **R** on meeting summit road. On reaching Bronze-Age Copper Mines and Halfway Station, retrace steps of outward route across high fields, back through Happy Valley.

# Horseshoe Falls The Velvet Hill

**4 miles (6.4km)** 2hrs 30min **Ascent:** 853ft (260m) ⚠

**Paths:** Field paths in valley and on hillside, 7 stiles

**Suggested map:** OS Explorer 255 Llangollen & Berwyn

**Grid reference:** SJ 198433

**Parking:** Picnic site and car park at Llantysilio Green on minor road north of Berwyn Station

## This walk on the Velvet Hill is probably one of the prettiest walks in North Wales.

**1** From car park walk down to road, turn **R** for few paces then descend some steps to back of **Chain Bridge Hotel**. Turn **R** to follow path between river and canal. Once through kissing gate at end of canal you traverse riverside fields past **Horseshoe Falls**. The falls are in fact a weir created by Thomas Telford to harness the waters of the Dee to feed and control the levels of the Llangollen and Ellesmere canals. Climb to **Llantysilio church** and on reaching road, turn **L** through hamlet of **Llantysilio** to junction.

**2** Go though 5-bar gate few paces along side road and climb along rutted track, with forest to your **L**, then climb north on high pastured hillside.

**3** Through gateway at top of field, path swings **R**, keeping parallel to top edge of another wood. The now narrow path descends to complex of cottages at **Pen-y-bryn**. After squeezing through ginnel to **R** of 1st

cottage, route follows tarmac drive out to Horseshoe Pass road at **Britannia Inn**.

**4** Turn **R** along road, then **R** again when you get to 1st junction. Go over stile on **L** to head south across 3 fields. Turn **R** along farm track then **L** past large stone-built house to arrive at narrow lane. Go **L** along this to meet Horseshoe Pass road again.

**5** Go over stile on **R-H** side of road (**'Velvet Hill'**) and ascend by quarry workings.

**6** Turn **R** along wide grassy track climbing steeply through bracken to reach ridge, where you turn **L** for summit. The view from here takes in the meandering Dee, the Afon Eglwyseg flowing beneath limestone terraces and **Valle Crucis abbey**.

**7** Descend southwards on narrow footpath to reach fence above some woods. Do not be tempted to cross (as many have done), but follow this fence down **L** to stile. Across stile go **R**, along path that leads back to car park and picnic site.

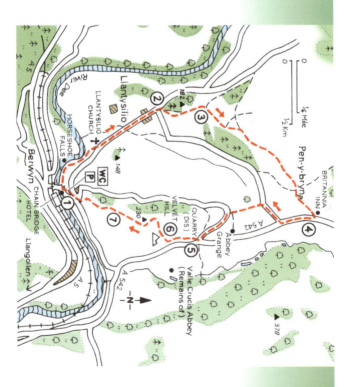

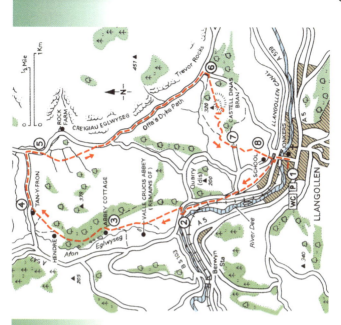

## Valle Crucis Idyllic Valle

**6 miles (9.7km)** 3hrs **Ascent:** 885ft (270m)

**Paths:** Tow path, farm tracks and field paths, 4 stiles

**Suggested map:** OS Explorer 255 Llangollen and Berwyn

**Grid reference:** SJ 216421

**Parking:** Small car park on A542 just to east of town centre

From the **Dee** to the **Eglwyseg**, this walk discovers a fascinating tapestry of history and landscape.

**1** Turn **L** out of car park to follow road to crossroads by Llangollen Bridge. Here turn **R**, then **L**, to café and on to canal tow path. Follow tow path westwards.

**2** After about 1 mile (1.6km) canal veers **L**. Leave tow path to cross canal on an ivy-clad bridge. Turn **R** along pavement of main road (A542). Cross road and take a farm track ('FP to **Valle Crucis**'). The track heads north past old abbey, where track ends. Continue on footpath, keeping fence to L.

**3** After crossing stile at **Abbey Cottage** turn **R** for few paces, then **L** to follow well-defined track through woodland. When you get to **Hendre** farm take **R-H** fork leading to minor road at **Tan-y-Fron**.

**4** Turn **R** along road, heading towards prominent cliffs of **Eglwyseg**, then **R** again, along lane that hugs foot of cliffs.

**5** A short stretch of tarmac to **Rock Farm** can be avoided by taking waymarked path that starts beyond gate and follows western edge of several fields before rejoining lane. Take **L-H** fork and stay with lane beneath cliffs.

**6** When you reach 2nd junction take **R-H** fork for few paces, then go through gate on **R**, on to waymarked footpath leading to **Castell Dinas Bran**. From crumbling west walls of castle descend on zig-zag path. Go around **R-H** side of little knoll at bottom of hill to reach high lane near house called Tirionfa.

**7** Follow lane southwards and then cross over stile into field. Trace **L-H** edge of field down to reach another high road.

**8** Across this, route continues down narrow enclosed ginnel, passing **school** before crossing road and then **Llangollen Canal** close to start of walk. Descend road down to Llangollen Bridge before turning **L**, back to car park.

# Prestatyn Mountains Meet Sea

**3 miles (4.8km)** 1hr 30min **Ascent:** 558ft (170m) ▲

**Paths:** Well-defined woodland paths and tracks

**Suggested map:** OS Explorer 264 Vale of Clwyd or 265 Clwydian Range

**Grid reference:** SJ 071821

**Parking:** Picnic site at foot of hill

A nature walk through wooded hillsides and limestone knolls and a coastal panorama from Prestatyn to Llandudno's Great Orme.

❶ Turn **R** out of car park and climb a few paces up steep lane. Turn **R** along public footpath marked with **Offa's Dyke National Trail** acorn sign. This enters an area of scrubby woodland with a wire fence to R, before climbing above some quarry workings. As footpath reaches high fields, ignore all paths off to L.

❷ The footpath continues along top edge of woods to **Tan-yr-Allt**, where it swings **L** to follow a footpath signposted to **Bryniau**. This rounds a little cove with some buildings in bottom, then swings to **L** again with Graig Fawr now peeping across another hollow.

❸ Go through a kissing gate on to a metalled lane and pass a house called Red Roofs. Turn **L** when you reach next junction, then **R** a few paces further on, to follow a lane rounding south side of **Graig Fawr**.

❹ Turn **R** through a gate on to **Graig Fawr** Estate

and follow a footpath leading to **trig point** on summit. Graig Fawr is an ideal place to picnic, either on the lush lawns or its gleaming white rock outcrops. Distant views from take in the North Wales coastline, the Vale of Clwyd and Carneddau mountains.

❺ Descend eastwards along a grassy path that weaves through bracken to a place where a line of wooden electricity pylons meets a stone wall bordering woodland. Locate stepped path that descends through woodland. Turn **L** at path junction and follow that through woods.

❻ Turn **R** along a **disused railway** track, before taking 2nd footpath on **R**, that crosses a field back towards **Prestatyn Hillside**. Turn L and follow a footpath into **Coed yr Esgob**, woods at foot of Prestatyn Hillside.

❼ Where path divides, take upper fork that joins Bishopwood Lane. Follow this back to car park and start of walk.

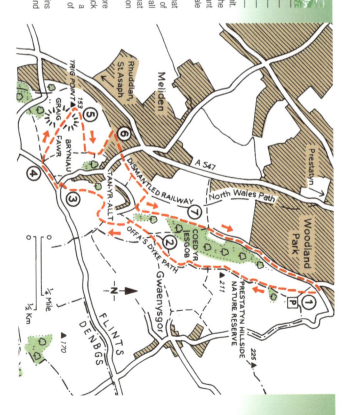

# Moel Famau The Mother Mountain

**8 miles (12.9km)** 5hrs **Ascent:** 1,608ft (490m) ⚠

**Paths:** Well-defined paths and forestry tracks, 9 stiles

**Suggested map:** OS Explorer 265 Clwydian Range

**Grid reference:** SJ 198625 **Parking:** Pay car park by Loggerheads Country Park Visitor Centre

**Note:** Route can be shortened by taking Moel Famau shuttle bus, which runs on Sundays (July to September) and bank holidays, from forestry car park to Loggerheads.

### Walk to the highest of the Clwydian Hills.

**1** Go past front of **Loggerheads Country Park Information Centre**, cross bridge over **Alun** and turn **L** along surfaced path through valley. Where path splits, follow route on **L** ('Leete Path').

**2** Look out for small and slippery-when-wet path on **L** beyond Alyn Kennels that takes you down to footbridge across river. Across this, path heads west, then staggers to **R** across a farm lane and climbs past farmhouse. Enclosed by thickets, it climbs to **R** of **Bryn Alyn** (cottage) to reach T-junction of country lanes. Go ahead and follow lane uphill, then turn **R** to follow track that passes **Ffrith** farm before swinging **L** to climb round pastured slopes of **Ffrith Mountain**. Take **L** fork in tracks (grid ref 177637).

**3** The route skirts spruce plantation and climbs to crossroads of tracks, marked by a tall waymarker post. Turn **L** here on wide path over undulating heather

slopes towards tower on top of **Moel Famau.**

**4** From summit, head southeast and go over stile at end of wall to follow wide track, marked with red-tipped waymarker posts, southeast along forest's edge. The track continues its descent through trees to meet roadside car park/picnic area ¾ mile (1.2km) east of **Bwlch Penbarra's** summit.

**5** Turn **L** along road, then turning **R** when at 1st junction, quiet lane leading to busy A494. Cross main road (care) and continue along hedge-lined lane staggered to **R**.

**6** A waymarked path on **L** heads northeast across fields towards banks of Alun. Don't cross river at bridge, but head north, through gateway and across more fields, keeping to **R** and above substantial stone-built house to meet **A494**. It's ½ mile (800m) to **Loggerheads Country Park** entrance, walk on verges and paths.

# Ceiriog Valley In the Beautiful Valley

**4½ miles (7.2km)** 2hrs 30min **Ascent:** 575ft (175m) ▲

**Paths:** Sketchy paths and farm tracks, 3 stiles

**Suggested map:** OS Explorer 255 Llangollen & Berwyn

**Grid reference:** SJ 157328

**Parking:** Roadside parking in village

**Discover an earthly haven in one of ancient Clwyd's truly green and pleasant valleys.**

**①** From **Hand Hotel**, take eastbound lane past church and uphill with conifer plantation on R and pastures of **Ceiriog** below L.

**②** At far end of plantation leave road for farm track on L. This ends at barn. Keep to R of barn and aim for gate beyond it. Through gate maintain your direction, over shoulder of grassy knoll, then aim for stile in fence ahead. Beyond this, route bends L very slightly, before going over another step stile.

**③** After crossing 2 streamlets, keep to field edge and to R of **Ty'n-y-fedw** farm. The track now enters woods. Take lower L fork, staying parallel to river.

**④** At far end of woods cross field, keeping roughly parallel with river, then aim for gate at top of field. Through gate, turn R to climb roughly southwest along enclosed farm road, which crosses country lane before continuing uphill through high pastures.

**⑤** At crossroads, turn R along green track – part of **Upper Ceiriog Way**. This heads southwest towards green hill known as Cefn Hir-fynydd.

**⑥** After about 300yds (274m) leave this track through gate on R. If you head west by R edge of rushy area and towards **Pen y Glog's** sparse crags, it will be easy to find small stile in next fence and then wooden gate on L soon afterwards. Go through gate then descend past rocks on L. The sheep track then levels out through bracken to pass beneath more rocks.

**⑦** A solitary wooden marker post acts as your guide to locate wide grassy track, which runs through valley of **Nant y Glog** and along low slopes of hill, **Pen y Glog**.

**⑧** After swinging **R** with lively stream, track terminates by lane to south of **Llanarmon Dyffryn Ceiriog**. Follow lane past several attractive cottages and village **school** to arrive by **Hand Hotel** in village square.

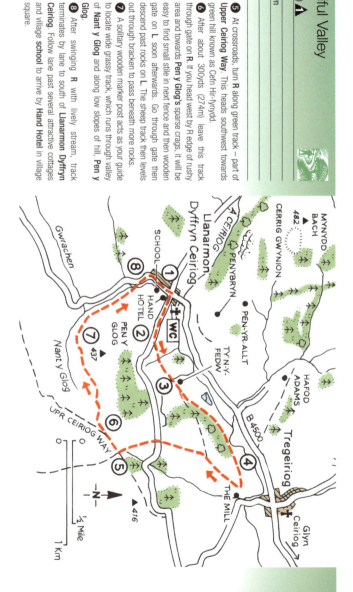

# Erddig A Magnificient Estate

**4 miles (6.4km)** 2hrs **Ascent:** 150ft (46m) ▲

**Paths:** Waymarked field and woodland paths and tracks 3 stiles

**Suggested map:** OS Explorer 265 Clwydian Range

**Grid reference:** SJ 346491

**Parking:** Small car park behind Kings Mill (on A525)

**Discover the Erddig Estate and a haven of tranquility just outside bustling centre of Wrexham.**

❶ From car park head west, following **River Clywedog** as it goes under road bridge. At other side turn **R** on grass path, then **L** alongside woods cloaking north slopes of valley. Go over stile and follow path into woods. This section is marked on maps as **Clywedog Trail**.

❷ Go through kissing gate and **L** along road. Turn **R** through gate at back of small car park and follow **L** of 2 paths to riverbank. Follow riverside path across fields, to south of bulrush-ringed lake.

❸ Go through gate to **R** of stone bridge, then turn **L** along track over bridge, keeping woods of Erddig to R. Near John Blakes Patent Hydraulic Ram go over stile on **L** and follow track south into woods. On reaching **Erddig Hall's** perimeter fence ignore path doubling back **L**, but follow path heading east by fence.

❹ Path ends at T-junction on far side of woods. Detour **R** for 50yds (46m) to get view of hall. This can be seen beyond some ornate wrought iron gates and long park-like gardens. (N.B. for those who want to pay to see the fine 17th-century hall continue to the south side entrance.) Return to T-junction. Head north along inside perimeter of woods then turn **R**. Go through kissing gate on to lane.

❺ Turn **L** along lane for a few paces and then cross over stile on **R-H** side of lane. Trace **L-H** field-edge to waymarker post and descend to another post at edge of woodland. Follow narrow path through woods, go over stile, down some steps to cross stream, then climb far banks to path overlooking bend in **River Clywedog**. Stay on path to continue above river, then, out of woods, turn **L** to cross over footbridge.

❻ Turn right along river banks to meet outward route at path going under road bridge and into grounds of Kings Mill.

## Greenfield Valley Grey Valley

**5 miles (8km)** 3hrs **Ascent:** 558ft (170m) ▲

**Paths:** Woodland paths and tracks, lanes, field paths and coastal embankment, 12 stiles

**Suggested map:** OS Explorer 265 Clwydian Range

**Grid reference:** SJ 196774

**Parking:** Just off A548 at Greenfield

**Following monks, martyrs and merchants.**

**①** Take footpath from back of car park on L-H side and follow it around **abbey**.

**②** Turn **L** between **information centre** and old schoolhouse on track passing Abbey Farm. Take **L** fork by brick walls of Abbey Wire Mill, following sign to Fishing Pool, a lily-covered pond.

**③** Beyond **Victoria Mill** take lower **R-H** fork, then turn **R** through iron gates to pass remains of Meadow Mill. Beyond mill turn **L** up steps, climbing up by weir and back on to main track.

**④** Turn **R** along track to pass above Hall's soft drinks factory and brick chimney. Go through kissing gate; turn **R** to road. Turn **L** to view **St Winefride's Chapel and Well**, then go back down road to **Royal Oak Inn**.

**⑤** Climb lane, called Green Bank, that begins from opposite side of road. At end of lane go over stile by gate and follow scrub-enshrouded footpath. At new housing estate path is dog-legged to **L** and continues

through trees to large open field.

**⑥** Go over stile and head diagonally, northwest, across field. Go through gap in far hedge and then over stile in bottom corner of next field. Continue ahead (still going northwest) through several more fields to join cart track, just short of tree-filled hollow of **Afon Marsiandwr**.

**⑦** Leave cart track where it swings to **R** for 2nd time and follow signed footpath through trees and down to banks of **Afon Marsiandwr**. After crossing stream, path climbs out of woods and crosses field to lane.

**⑧** Turn **R** along lane following it down to coast road. Cross busy road with care. The continuing footpath to seashore is immediately opposite, over step stile. Cross railway track, again with care, and continue to inner flood embankments and turn **R**.

**⑨** The footpath comes out by Greenfield Harbour. Turn **R** along lane back in to **Greenfield**. Turn **L** to return to car park.

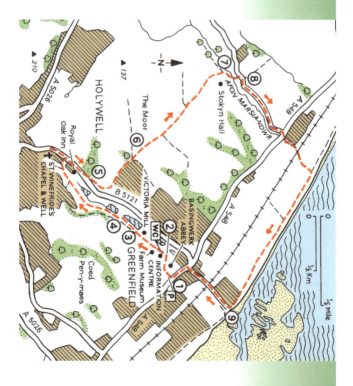

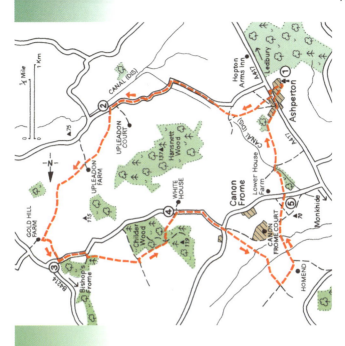

# Ashperton Hereford's Lost Canal

**7¾ miles (12.5km)** 3hrs 30min **Ascent:** 260ft (79m) ⚠

**Paths:** Field and woodland paths, minor roads, at least 35 stiles

**Suggested map:** OS Explorer 202 Leominster & Bromyard

**Grid reference:** SO 642415

**Parking:** St Bartholomew's Church, Ashperton

### Along an old waterway, now being restored.

**①** From car park take 'forty shillings' gate, behind houses. (For 10 paces path is in a garden!) Join track to **A417**. Turn **L**, then **R**, beside driveway. Follow fingerpost across meadows for 600yds (549m). Find gate by cricket net. Veer **R**. Cross driveway down field. Join Haywood Lane near house. Turn **L**. Follow this for 1 mile (1.6km). Find stile on **L** just beyond gate, 100yds (91m) after driveway to **Upleadon Court**.

**②** Cross arable fields and ditch, then **Upleadon Farm's** driveway. Aim for **L-H** corner. Skirt woodland to L, later striking **L** (waymarked) up huge field. At **Gold Hill Farm** go **R** of tall shed. Behind this, turn **L** then briefly up and **R**. Follow boundary to road.

**③** Turn **L** for ¼ mile (400m). Where road turns **L** continue for ½ mile (800m), initially beside wood. Over rotting plank turn **L** but in 25yds (23m) turn **R**. After 500yds (457m) enter trees. On leaving them strike half **R** for **White House**.

**④** Turn **R** along road. At junction, take footpath opposite (ditch on R). (Beware of hitting your head on horizontal tree trunk just after single-plank footbridge.) Walk 700yds (640m) across fields, over 3 footbridges and under power lines, passing through gap to stile, but do not cross – note 3 waymarkers on its far side. Turn **L**, heading towards old orchards. Just beyond **Homend** find stile in far **L-H** corner, shielded by ash and elder. Turn **L**, soon moving **R** to double gates flanking wide concrete bridge. After avenue keep ahead, eventually veering **R**. Go 550yds (503m), crossing driveway to **Canon Frome Court**, then another track, finally reaching road by spinney.

**⑤** Cross road; walk to canal. Turn **L**. In 140yds (128m) turn **R**, over canal. Veer **L** and uphill, finding large oak in top **L-H** corner. Keep this line despite field boundary shortly curving away. At copse turn **R**, later moving **L** into indistinct lane. Village hall heralds **A417**. Turn **L**, along pavement then **R** to **church**.

# Frome Valley Two Churches

**4¾ miles (7.7km)** 2hrs 30min **Ascent:** 475ft (145m) ▲

**Paths:** Field paths, dirt tracks, lanes and minor roads, 14 stiles

**Suggested map:** OS Explorer 202 Leominster & Bromyard

**Grid reference:** SO 679502

**Parking:** Roadside just before grassy lane to Acton Beauchamp's church – please tuck in tightly

You'll discover secluded churches and special wild service trees set amid pastures on this easy ramble.

**❶** Leave churchyard by iron gate in top corner. Soon enter orchard. Skirt round to **R**, passing outbuildings of **Church House Farm** and then down to pass behind tall barns. Now orchard track ascends. When 110yds (100m) beyond power lines, at corner of plantation, turn **L** (blue waymarker), to walk between orchard rows. At end turn **L**. In roughly 160yds (146m), well before power lines and just before trees shielding pond, go **R**. Soon you'll have hedge on your **L**, reach gate and stile of 3 railway sleepers.

**❷** Once through **Halletshill Coppice** drop straight down to footbridge. Now go straight up bank, swapping hedge sides, to minor road. Turn **R**. Take the opportunity to visit the **church**. You will notice that the stonework is of a similar vintage to that in **Acton Beauchamp** – Norman and 13th-century. Return to

road and turn **R**. At entrance to **The Hawkins** take stile, then follow waymarkers across track to skirt this farm. Now head down pastures to cross footbridge over **Linton Brook**.

**❸** Turn **L**, walking beside **Linton Brook** for ⅝ mile (1km), to road. Turn **L** for 160yds (146m). Turn **R**. Now driveway to **Upper Venn Farm** runs for ½ mile (800m). Just before farm buildings move **L**, to stile roughly 70yds (64m) along edge of field from farm.

**❹** Cross field diagonally, to gate in **L** hedge. Turn **L** across field, aiming slightly uphill, beside residual mature oaks. You'll find stile beyond electricity pole. Pick up rough track to **The Venn**. Admire its cream walls and exposed timbers and then turn away, along drive. Follow this down to minor road.

**❺** Turn **L**, passing **Frome Valley Vineyard** on a sharp bend. At crossroads go straight over. Climbing this quite steep lane, **Church of St Giles** comes into view. Take 1st turning on **L** to return to your car.

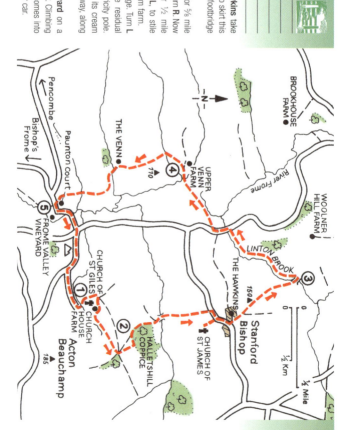

# Hereford Historic Streets

2¾ miles (4.4km) 1hr 45min **Ascent:** Negligible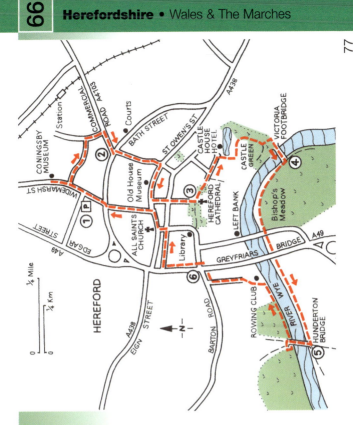

**Paths:** City streets, riverside path and tracks

**Suggested map:** OS Explorer 189 Hereford & Ross-on-Wye

**Grid reference:** SO 510403

**Parking:** Garrick House long-stay, pay-and-display multi-storey car park, Widemarsh Street

**Note:** Several busy junctions without subways – care needed

### Around a charming medieval city.

❶ Turn **L** out of car park. After 150yds (137m) is Coningsby Hospital, now **Coningsby Museum**. Go back short way to walk along Coningsby Street, to T-junction. Turn **R** on Monkmoor Street. Turn **R** into **Commercial Road**. At Blueschool Street junction is city wall, while on near side are magistrates' courts.

❷ Cross Commercial Road then **Bath Street**. Follow Union Street. Go **R** to High Town. Go **L** down Church Street, to **Hereford Cathedral** (TIC on R).

❸ Go **L**, beside cathedral, passing stonemasons' workshop. Go along Castle Street. Shortly before **Castle House Hotel** turn **R** to **Castle Green**. Hug railings on L, beside Castle Pool (part of original moat), to walk above green and Nelson Column (1809). Zigzag down to cross **Victoria Footbridge**.

❹ Turn **R** (or L for extended riverside stroll) passing putting green, tennis courts and wood carving.

Keeping on south side of river – opposite **Left Bank** complex – cross St Martin's Street to go under **Greyfriars Bridge**, continuing to **Hunderton Bridge**.

❺ Cross old railway bridge. When **River Wye** floods, this footway/cycleway provides emergency vehicular access. Take steps down back towards city. Skirt **rowing club**, then walk up Greyfriars Avenue. Just before junction go half **R** across car park to go through pedestrian subway. (But go **R**, through car subway, to see city wall.) Brick building ahead is built on city wall. Go up steps. Cross St Nicholas' Street (take care).

❻ As you begin along Victoria Street, you'll see single tree. A few paces beyond it, 10ft (3m) up in wall, is a cannon ball, which was probably embedded there during the siege of **Hereford** in 1645. Go along West Street to Broad Street. Turn **L**. Walk towards **All Saints Church**. Turn **R** then **L**, down **Widemarsh Street** to car park.

# Coppet Hill Beside the River Wye

**Paths:** Quiet lanes, riverside meadows, woodland paths, 2 stiles
**Suggested map:** OS Explorer OL14 Wye Valley & Forest of Dean
**Grid reference:** SO 575196
**Parking:** Goodrich Castle car park open daily 9:30am to 7pm

**A peaceful walk with fine views.**

**1** Walk back to castle access road junction; turn **L**. In 125yds (114m) cross bridge over **B4229**.

**2** Go up further 400yds (366m). Ignore another road branching off to R, and go on just a few paces – there are 3 low wooden posts to your **L**.

**3** Opposite, between 2 roads, sign ('**Coppet Hill** Nature Reserve') indicates return route. Go ½ mile (800m) up this dead end, to cattle grid. Here, at brow, woods give way to parkland. Go ahead for 275yds (251m) to single horse chestnut tree at **R** turn.

**4** Continue for 400yds (366m), bending **L** and dipping down, along road. It curves **R** slightly, while gravel track goes up ramp and slightly **L**.

**5** Curve **R**. Ignore pillared driveway but go down **youth hostel's** driveway. At its entrance gate take footpath that runs initially parallel to it. Go down wooden steps and along sometimes muddy path to reach T-junction beside **River Wye**.

**6** Turn **R**, following Wye Valley Walk (turn **L** to visit **church** first). Within ¼ mile (400m) you'll reach old, iron girder railway bridge, which now carries Wye Valley Walk across river, but stay this side, passing underneath bridge. After walking 125yds (114m) look out for 6 wooden steps down to **L** at fork.

**7** Take steps, to remain close to river. Continue for about 1¼ miles (2km). Enter **Coldwell Wood** to walk beside river for further ¼ mile (400m). On leaving, keep by river in preference to path that follows woodland's edge. In about 350yds (320m) you'll reach stile beside fallen willow.

**8** Turn **R** ('**Coppet Hill**'). Soon begin arduous woodland ascent. Eventually you'll have some fine views. Path levels, later rising to **The Folly**, then goes down (not up) to triangulation point. Follow clear green sward ahead, becoming narrow rut then stepped path, down to road, close to Point **3**. Retrace your steps to castle car park.

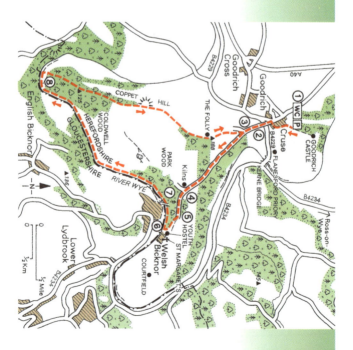

# Aymestrey Rocks of Ages

**4¾ miles (7.7km)** 2hrs 30min **Ascent:** 525ft (160m) ▲

**Paths:** Good tracks, field paths, minor roads, steep woodland sections, 11 stiles

**Suggested map:** OS Explorer 203 Ludlow

**Grid reference:** SO426658

**Parking:** At old quarry entrance, on east side of A4110, ¼ mile (400m) north of Aymestrey Bridge

## Around a redeveloped quarry now used for grazing and woodland.

❶ Walk up access road for almost ½ mile (800m), until beyond garden of house and just before junction of tracks. Note stile on R – your route returns over this.

❷ Go 30yds (27m) further and turn **L**, passing house with stone wall relic in its garden. Continue, through **Yatton**, to T-junction. Turn **L** to **A4110**. Cross to stile, walking along **L-H** field edge. Through gate go forward then skirt round **R** edge of oak and ash embankment, to find corner stile. Walk up **L** edge of field but, at brow, where it bends for 70yds (64m) to corner, slip **L** through gap in hedge to walk along its other side. Within 60yds (55m) you will be on clear path, steeply down through woodland, ravine on your **L**. Join driveway of **River Bow**, to minor road.

❸ Turn **L** here, joining **Mortimer Trail**. Continue along riverside lane for nearly ¾ mile (1.2km), to reach **A4110**. Cross then walk for 25yds (23m) to **R**.

(**Riverside Inn** is 175yds/160m further.) Take raised green track, heading for hills. Then go diagonally across 2 fields, to stile and wooden steps.

❹ Ascend steeply through trees. Leave by stile, to cross 2 meadows diagonally. Take stile on **R** to walk along **L-H** edge of field, still heading downhill. At trees turn **L**. Soon reach tarmac road. Turn **L** along road, now going back uphill. Beyond **Hill Farm**, enter Croft Estate. Walk along gravel track. After 110yds (100m) ignore R fork but, 550yds (503m) further on, you must leave it. This spot is identified by end to deciduous trees on **L** and **Mortimer Trail** marker post on wide ride between larches and evergreens on R.

❺ Turn **L** (no signpost). Within 110yds (100m) go half **R** and more steeply down. Within 250yds (229m) look out for modern wooden gate, waymarked, leading out of woods. Walk along its **R-H** edge (and beside small plantation). At far corner, within field, turn **L** to Point ❷. Retrace your steps to start.

# Harley's Mountain Bracing Air

**3¾ miles (6km)** 2hrs 15min **Ascent:** 755ft (230m) ▲ ▲

**Paths:** Meadows, field paths, woodland tracks with roots, 10 stiles

**Suggested map:** OS Explorer 201 Knighton & Presteigne

**Grid reference:** SO 364672

**Parking:** At St Michael's Church, Lingen (tuck in well)

**A brisk walk in farming country.**

**❶** Walk away from **church**; cross to take minor road ('Willey'). At 1st bend, follow fingerpost directly ahead. Climb over difficult gate beside small corrugated shed; walk by paddock edge, reaching lane in trees.

**❷** Strike up field, passing dead oak. Follow waymarker up and slightly **R**. In corner, negotiate rusty gate between better ones. At derelict **Mynde Farm** skirt **L**, around 2 collapsed buildings. Find gate on **R** behind low building.

**❸** Go down and up meadow to stile. Veer **L**, passing beside **Mountain Buildings** on rutted, rocky track. After 160yds (146m) enter field. Take line diagonally across field (but if ridged with potatoes, or other crop, follow 2 field edges **L**) then keep that line, now with hedge **L**. Take track along ridge to gate with pool to **R** (dry in summer). Above and behind is trig point.

**❹** Turn **L**, initially preferring L-H field edge to lane (overgrown). Descend for 650yds (594m). At bottom move **L**, to small gate. Through trees, shortly emerge close to **The Red House**. Keep ahead, finding narrow path within trees, **R** of garage and beside hedge. Within 40yds (37m) negotiate metal gate. Don't be tempted down; instead move **L**, beside wire fence for just a few paces, then, maintaining fence's line, proceed to walk below narrow ridge on faint tractor track for 100yds (91m). When ground ahead drops steeply into dell turn half **L**, to walk down woody edge of meadow. In 2nd meadow, where trees bulge out to **L**, dive back into woodland – (waymarker on oak).

**❺** Go ahead, sometimes boggy, in woodland then pasture, for ½ mile (800m). At wobbly silver-grey gate drop **L** 10ft (3m) to waymarked stile into once pollarded, streamside lane. Reach road.

**❻** Turn **L**. After 450yds (411m), on bend, go straight down field to hedge beside farm buildings. Find stile in **L** corner. Go ahead, to stile that gives on to village road – take care! Turn **R** to see **church** before reaching car.

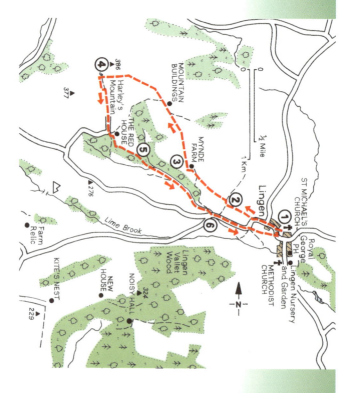

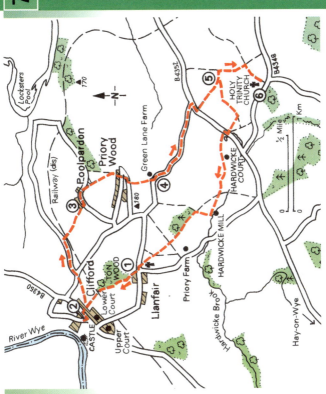

## Clifford Original Settlement

**5½ miles (8.8km)** 2hrs 30min **Ascent:** 560ft (171m) **2**

**Paths:** Field paths and lanes, awkward embankment, over 30 stiles

**Suggested map:** OS Explorer 201 Knighton & Presteigne

**Grid reference:** SO 251450 **Parking:** Roadside parking at St Mary's Church, Llanfair

**A 'backwater' of the River Wye.**

**1** Just after road junction at corner of churchyard, take steps on **R**. Yellow arrows indicate route. Leave **Ton Wood** by gate on **L**, beside wire game-breeding enclosure. More arrows lead across old railway towards **Clifford**. Leave last meadow beside house.

**2** Walk to road. Turn **L** then **R** for **castle**. Retrace your steps to Point **2**. Take arrow pointing to oaks. At tarmac beyond follow 'Unsuitable for heavy goods vehicles'. On **R**, after 440yds (402m) find stile (hidden) and go up steep steps – easier is metal gate 30yds (27m) before stile. Across this green strip scramble down and up railway embankment. Halfway up field switch hedge from your **L** to **R**. Find stile behind derelict harvester. Wooded path soon reaches lane.

**3** Turn **L** in 230yds (210m), through garden, strike **R**, to stile behind 6 hawthorns in dip. Through garden, take rough track joining 2 tarmac lanes. Turn **R** for 30 paces. Waymarker points towards stile in trees. Go down this field to meet lane.

**4** Turn **L**; continue for ½ mile (800m) to B4352. Turn **R**. In 70yds (64m) cross to stile into meadow. Aim to **R** of trees on skyline then stile by house.

**5** Walk through garden. Take bridleway, **R**. After leafy interlude join stony track, but within 160yds (146m), where footpath crosses, turn **R**, to reach **Holy Trinity Church.**

**6** Retrace your steps to Point **5**. Go diagonally **L** to stile hidden by hedge. Turn **R**, around 2 sides of field. In next turn **R**, along field edge. Take driveway near by. At **Hardwicke Court** step around wall to walk **R** beside building, down path on lawn. At bottom, through small gate, maintain line, although 'Road Used as a Public Path' is obliterated. At farm gate keep ahead, past gigantic oak, to find wicket gate – 'RUPP' becomes more defined. Don't take waymarked stile 40yds (37m) to **R**. At **Hardwicke Mill** go into garden. Leave by stile on **R**. Ascend field edge, striking **L** at trees. Having skirted to **R** of house, you'll see **St Mary's Church** across fields ahead. Head for church.

**6 miles (9.7km)** 3hrs **Ascent:** 1,165ft (355m) ▲

**Paths:** Minor lanes, good tracks, meadows, couple of short but severe descents over grass, 24 stiles

**Suggested map:** OS Explorer 201 Knighton & Presteigne or OL13 Brecon Beacons (East)

**Grid reference:** SO 313416 (on Explorer 201) **Parking:** Car park beside Dorstone Post Office

### Across a heavenly landscape.

**1** Go down near side village green but turn **R** (not to church, passing houses. At lane end turn **L**, passing D'Or Produce Ltd. At **B4348** care is required. Continue, bridging **River Dore**. Be sure to switch sides before road bends severely **R**. Follow driveway towards **Fayre Way Stud Farm**. Clearly waymarked route across pastures leads up to **Arthur's Stone**.

**2** Beyond **Arthur's Stone** take route signed by fingerpost. Cross 2nd field diagonally. Follow **L** side of fence to stile **L** of the corner. After 2 fields descend very steeply on grass beside larches. Keep beside hedge to find awkward stile. Take lane but skirt **R** of **Finestreet Farm** using several stiles. In another steep meadow find stile below and **L** of massive oak with fallen one beside it. Cross field diagonally, to pass beside timber-framed house. Beyond is **Bredwardine**.

**3** Cross road carefully. In 80yds (73m) avenue leads to **St Andrew's Church**. At very end, stile and waymarkers lead to Bredwardine's bridge.

**4** Go back to Point **3**. Take '25%' gradient road beside **Red Lion Hotel**. Go 700yds (640m) up lane, including steepest section, to just before **Hill Cottage**. Fingerpost points **R**, and behind you is '1 in 4' sign.

**5** Keep ahead, ignoring **R** turn after 160yds (146m). When road rises sharply after stream, find gate **R**, just past house (**'Finestreet Dingle'**). Now ascend dell (also called Finestreet Dingle) guided by blue arrows. In front of house turn **L** then **L** again, to skirt plantation. Row of hawthorns points to stile near brow. Tackle awkward gate near scrawny pines, keeping this line to minor road. Turn **R**. In 325yds (297m) turn **L** ('20%'). After another 325yds (297m) find fingerpost, hidden behind holly tree.

**6** Soon join track visible ahead. Continue to and through **Llan Farm**. However, 220yds (201m) beyond it, take diagonal footpath (not old lane, **R**). Cross sunken lane, old **railway**, then village playing fields to reach road near church. Cross then skirt **R** of churchyard, along fenced path, to village green.

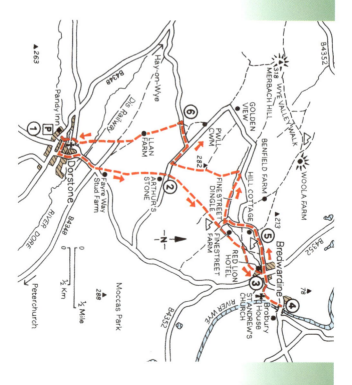

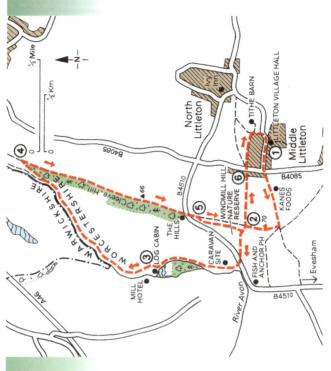

# Cleeve Hill A Fruity Route

**4½ miles (7.2km)** 2hrs **Ascent:** 225ft (69m) ▲

**Paths:** Paths across fields, stony tracks and village roads, 8 stiles

**Suggested map:** OS Explorer 205 Stratford-upon-Avon & Evesham

**Grid reference:** SP 077469

**Parking:** Outside Littleton Village Hall, School Lane, Middle Littleton (tithe barn parking for visitors only)

**Walking in Victoria plum country.**

❶ Walk westwards up School Lane to B4085, here called Cleeve Road. Cross diagonally **L** to take rutted, stony track, screened by hedgerow from **Kanes Foods**. At junction of tracks turn **R** to pass beside gate, following blue arrow. After 328yds (300m) reach opening **R** and line of plum trees making field boundary, on **L** is stile.

❷ Cross it, entering Worcestershire Wildlife Trust's **Windmill Hill Nature Reserve**. Descend, ignoring crossing tracks, to another stile and across 1 field to B4510. Follow footpath ('Cleeve Prior') through **caravan site**. (Keep on road for 220yds/201m for **Fish and Anchor**.) Take stile out of caravan park to walk on stone track beside river.

❸ At fenced log cabin with lanterns and basketball net, move to **R** to take double-stiled footbridge – don't be deterred by sign 'OPAC Private Fishing' – and resume riverside stroll. Continue through mostly

ungated pastures. Go through small iron gate, leave river by taking **R-H** fork. Ascend through trees to clearing and path junction.

❹ Turn **R**, back on yourself, soon walking into trees again, to follow bridleway. In just under 1 mile (1.6km) B4510 cuts through hill, beside **The Hills**. Cross to fingerpost, but follow path for just 75yds (69m).

❺ Climb stile into nature reserve here, and follow waymarked, contouring path. After 440yds (402m) you'll recognise your outward route. Turn **L** here, up bank, retracing your steps for just 30yds (27m), to Point ❷. Once at top go straight across, walking with line of plum trees on your **L**. When this ends, maintain this direction to B4085, **tithe barn** making clear objective ahead.

❻ Cross road and go straight ahead. Before young trees take stile or gate to **R**. In 15yds (14m) turn **L** to visit tithe barn, or turn **R** to reach village road. Turn **R** again, shortly to start.

# Tardebigge The Ups and Downs

5½ miles (8.8km) 2hrs 30min **Ascent:** 295ft (90m) ▲

**Paths:** Tow path, pastures, field paths and minor lanes, 21 stiles

**Suggested map:** OS Explorer 204 Worcester & Droitwich Spa

**Grid reference:** SO 974682

**Parking:** Limited space, so park tightly and considerately, on north and east side of road bridge

**Visit Worcestershire's famous big wet steps.**

**①** Cross bridge No 51 and turn **L**, taking tow path on south side. Follow this until about 15yds (14m) before next bridge – No 52.

**②** Turn **R** here, into trees, then down field. Cross double-stiled footbridge among trees then keep ahead, over driveway to **Patchetts Farm**. Skirt copse to **L**, then another stile and 2-plank bridge. Cross 2 fields, keeping hedge on your **L**. You will reach gate on your **L**, close to broken oak tree with substantial girth.

**③** Turn **R**. Within 110yds (100m) go through gate ahead (no waymarker), ignoring gate to **L**. Go a quarter **R** (or skirt crops) to find stile. Retain this diagonal line to cross footbridge of 3 planks, then find rickety, narrow stile in next field's corner. Walk with hedge on your **L** to reach minor road junction. Turn **R** for 55yds (50m). Turn **L** to walk across 3 more fields to dilapidated metal gate. Now take **R-H** field edge to reach minor road.

**④** Turn **R**. Follow this for ½ mile (800m) to **Lower Bentley Farm's** driveway. Go 140yds (128m) further, to fingerpost on **R**. Cross pastures by gaps in hedgerows, later with hedge on your **L**, but veer to stile in **R-H** corner at end. Cross this, then double stile, go three-quarters **L** to road.

**⑤** Turn **R**, and in 75yds (69m) turn **L**. Here, beyond awkward ditch, is new kissing gate with latch. Cross pastures easily towards **Orchard Farm**, but then turn **R**, away from it. Over corner stile go straight ahead. At double stile (across ditch) go half **L**, and at gap in hedge turn **R**. Now turn **L** without gaining height for 650yds (594m), aiming to **L** of black-and-white house, for stile and gate. In 80yds (73m) reach road.

**⑥** Turn **R**. At T-junction turn **L**. Join canal tow path this side of Stoke Pound Bridge. (The **Queen's Head** is on other side). Now you have over ¾ mile (1.2km) to return to your car at road bridge, approximately mid-way up **Tardebigge Flight**.

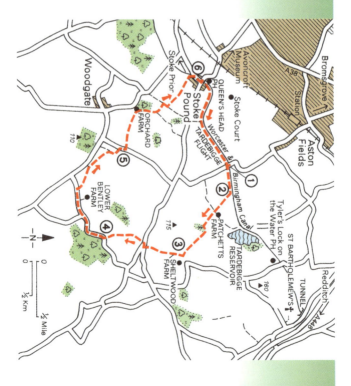

# Hanbury Hall The Ice Houses

**4¾ miles (7.7km)** 2hrs 15min **Ascent:** 250ft (76m)

**Paths:** Meadows, tracks and easy woodland paths, 17 stiles

**Suggested map:** OS Explorer 204 Worcester & Droitwich Spa

**Grid reference:** SO 957652

**Parking:** Piper's Hill car park, on B4091 between Stoke Works and Hanbury (fast road and no sign)

## A stroll around an estate park.

**1** From bottom of car park, follow driveway to **Knotts Farm**. Go ahead on **L-H** (1 of 2 parallel paths). 350yds (320m) after farm reach track at fingerpost.

**2** Keep ahead, with field boundary on L. Ascending towards **church**, reach stake with 2 waymarkers.

**3** Fork **L**, soon passing spinney, then losing height across meadow. Take care as stile and steps here spill you straight on to minor but fast road. Cross then go beside **school**. Ahead, when 20yds (18m) before stile out of 3rd field, turn **R**, aiming just to L of young, fenced oak. Cross wobbly stile. In 70yds (64m) cross footbridge on **L**. Cross 2 stiles to Pumphouse Lane.

**4** Turn **R**. Take stile and gate close to black-and-white **Grumbleground Cottage**. In 40yds (37m) cross 3-plank footbridge. Ascend slightly, in line with electricity poles. After 2 fields turn **R**, alongside wire fence. Reach road.

**5** Cross road to footpath opposite. At stile go half **L**,

guided by solitary, fenced conifer. Pass close to **Hanbury Hall's** entrance, easing away from perimeter wall to cross large field to corner.

**6** Ignore minor road, turning immediately **R**. Hug boundary fence of coppice. Continue down **R-H** field edge. At junction turn **R** at National Trust sign, into this former deer park. After just 50yds (46m), at small drainage ditch, edge **R**, along slight green hollow. After another 110yds (100m), where it curves **R**, leave hollow to keep line. Aim for stile about 300yds (274m) away, to **L** of clump of fenced trees, which hides round pond. Maintain this line going up incline – **Hanbury church** is seen on **L** – to reach tarmac driveway.

**7** Turn **L**. When it curves **R** go straight ahead to walk in oak avenue. Keep this line for 700yds (640m), to minor road. Turn **R**, then **L** up to church. In churchyard walk round perimeter, down to kissing gate. Shortly rejoin outward route at Point **3**. Remember to go **L**, into woods, at Point **2**.

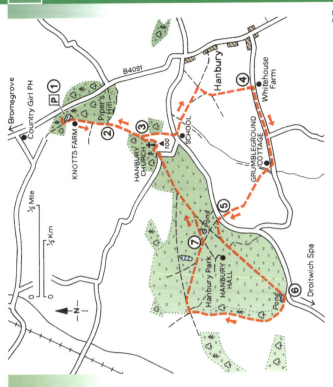

# Clent Hills A Treat in Springtime

3½ miles (5.7km) 2hrs **Ascent:** 660ft (200m) ▲

**Paths:** Woodland paths (sometimes muddy), tracks, 8 stiles

**Suggested map:** OS Explorer 219 Wolverhampton & Dudley

**Grid reference:** SO 938808

**Parking:** National Trust pay-and-display car park, Nimmings Wood

A brief circuit of the most visited hills in Worcestershire and where, in spring, fields of **oilseed flood the landscape with colour.**

**1** Return to car park entrance and turn **R** for few paces. Cross road to stile and take **L-H** of 2 options. Immediately you'll see striking urban panorama. Descend steadily but, at cylindrical wooden post, turn **R** (with waymarker). Continue across fields, probably populated with horses, until kissing gate. Here take forward option (not R fork), to reach churchyard of **St Kenelm's** in Romsley parish. It may appear to be 'overgrown' since it is managed like a traditional hay meadow.

**2** Leave by lychgate. Turn **L** along road for short distance, then **R** at T-junction. In about 125yds (114m) take waymarked path at driveway to **The Wesleys** to ascend gently. Turn **L** on to tarmac road. Ignore L turn but, just 30yds (27m) beyond it, take muddy, narrow path into woodland up on **R**, angled

away from road and not signposted. Emerge from trees to trig point on **Walton Hill**. Turn **L**, taking **R-H** of 2 options. Follow this for ¾ mile (1.2km) until just 10yds (9m) beyond National Trust marker post. Here take **R-H** fork to stile. Go steeply down 2 meadows to road beside **Church of St Leonard's** in **Clent**.

**3** Turn **R** then **R** again. At Church View Cottage, opposite church's driveway, turn **L** in 125yds (114m) take upper, **L** fork. In 90yds (82m), at crossing, go **L**. After further 100yds (91m) ignore options to turn **R** or half **R**. Proceed for further 120yds (110m). Do not climb stile on your L but go straight on, soon ascending steeply up wooden steps. After another 100yds (91m) you'll emerge from trees. Now cross track then turn **R**.

**4** Keep on this broad, open path, passing close to (or viewing) a toposcope beside four standing stones. Maintain this line to descend in woodland to road. Just on L is car park.

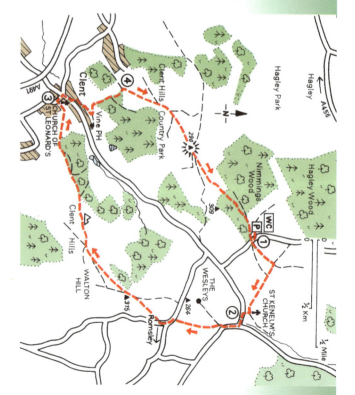

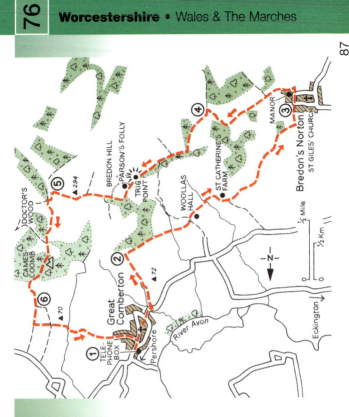

# Bredon Hill Perry Country

7½ miles (12.1km) 3hrs 30min **Ascent:** 1,115ft (340m) ▲

**Paths:** Tracks, woodland paths, bridleways, minor lanes, 11 stiles

**Suggested map:** OS Explorer 190 Malvern Hills & Bredon Hill

**Grid reference:** SO 955423 **Parking:** Roadside parking, Great Comberton village

**A walk through perry country.**

**1** Begin by **telephone box** in **Great Comberton**. Follow Church Street. Go through churchyard; leave by gate. At road go down stem of T-junction. In dip find stile. Ascend 2 fields, with stream on your L. After 100yds (91m) in 3rd field there is a signpost.

**2** Turn **R**, initially beside trees. Soon good farm track strikes across meadow. Follow waymarkers for next 1½ miles (2.4km), taking gravel driveway beside **Woollas Hall** and skirting **St Catherine's Farm**. Take hard track, later tarmac, down into **Bredon's Norton**. After first few houses reach junction.

**3** Keep ahead for 100yds (91m) to junction. Turn **R** if visiting **St Giles' Church**; otherwise go ahead again, then round **L** bend. Go into field, to **R** of 2 buildings – waymarker on telegraph pole. Now follow track steadily upwards, through several gates, eventually swinging southeast, for at least ¾ mile (1.2km). Less than 100yds (91m) beyond single marker post reach T-junction with 'no right of way' ahead.

**4** Turn **L**. Soon go half **R** along field edge, then **R** to walk along wooded escarpment ridge, before open field leads to **triangulation pillar**. Continue through fortifications and past 18th-century tower, **Parson's Folly**. Follow escarpment eastwards. Pass small plantation, then follow wire fence, slightly descending, for over ¼ mile (400m), to wood.

**5** Don't enter wood; turn **L**, beside it. Within 150yds (137m), bend **R** to junction. Turn **L**, down green hollow. At **Doctor's Wood** veer **L** to cross oddly level field (note absence of contours on suggested map). Descend steeply through **Cames Coomb**, along wide, well-horsed path. Briefly follow level forestry road, then leave trees, descending on scalpings track for 400yds (366m) to path junction.

**6** Walk a further 375yds (343m) on good track to find path on **L**, initially between 2 hedges. When it ends keep ahead. Keep this general line – later hard track – back into **Great Comberton**. Turn **R** to telephone box.

# Droitwich Spa Salt into Silver

**5¾ miles (9.2km)** 2hrs 30min **Ascent:** 230ft (70m) ▲

**Paths:** Pavements, field paths, stony tracks, 6 stiles

**Suggested map:** OS Explorer 204 Worcester & Droitwich Spa

**Grid reference:** SO 898631

**Parking:** Long-stay pay-and-display between Heritage Way and Saltway (follow signs for 'Brine Baths')

**An historic salt-making town.**

**1** From **TIC**, go along Victoria Square. Cross Heritage Way into Ombersley Street East. When it bends keep ahead, passing magistrates' court. After underpass proceed to St Nicholas's Church. Go round churchyard to take another underpass. Turn **L**. Take road over railway to mini-roundabout, filtering **R** to go through 3rd underpass. Walk for 65yds (60m) to fence corner, near lamppost. Turn **L**. In 30yds (27m) turn **R**. At bottom of this cul-de-sac, Westmead Close, turn **L**. Soon take Ledwych Close, on **R**. At canal you have left Droitwich Spa.

**2** Turn **L**. At bridge turn **R**; continue. Turn **L** just after A38 bridge. In 110yds (100m) reach **Westwood House** slip road. Facing allotments, take kissing gate to **L**. Beyond woodland go across several fields. Within 500yds (457m) at 2nd driveway is junction.

**3** Turn sharply **R**. Electric fencing leads between paddocks then veer **L** to walk briefly through **Nunnery Wood**. Aim for 2 gateposts beside tree. Keep ahead for ½ mile (800m), beside big **dairy** on **L**, then curving **L** past **industrial estate** to reach Doverdale Lane.

**4** Turn **R** on lane. Just before '30' speed-limit sign, fork **L**. Cross A442. Go through **Hampton Lovett** to **St Mary's Church**. Take meadow path under railway. In 140yds (128m), at footbridge, bear **R**, along field edge. Maintain direction for over ½ mile (800m), walking in trees beside **Highstank Pool** when fence allows. Track leads to evergreens shielding golf tee.

**5** Cross vast field, then aim slightly **L** to metal gate. Follow road under A38 into housing estate. Find path running between Nos 49 and 53. Go through 2 kissing gates flanking level crossing. Turn **L** to pass Gardeners Arms. In 20yds (18m) turn **R** over **River Salwarpe**, into Vines Park. Veer **L** to cross the Droitwich Canal. Over B4090, follow Gurney Lane to High Street – ahead is **Spats Coffee House**. Turn **R**, passing Tower Hill, then **L** into St Andrew's Street.

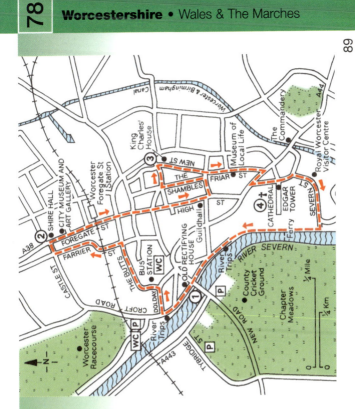

# Worcester City Sights and Smells

2½ miles (4km) 1hr 30min **Ascent:** Negligible ⚠

**Paths:** City streets and tarmac riverside path

**Suggested map:** OS Explorer 204 Worcester & Droitwich Spa

**Grid reference:** SO 846548

**Parking:** Long-stay pay-and-display car parks at New Road, Tybridge Street and Croft Road

A town walk in Worcester, known for Sir Edward Elgar, its battle, its porcelain, its racecourse and its sauce.

**①** The described route begins at the city side of the road bridge, but you can pick it up anywhere – at The Commandery or the Guildhall, for example – depending on where you have parked. Turn **L**, along North Parade, passing **Old Rectifying House** (wine bar). Turn **R** up **Dolday**, then **L**, in front of **bus station**, along **The Butts**. Turn **L** along **Farrier Street**, **R** into **Castle Street**, reaching northern extremity of route at its junction with Foregate Street.

**②** Go **R** along **Foregate Street**, passing **Shire Hall** and **City Museum and Art Gallery**, continuing along The Cross and into pedestrianised area called **High Street**. Turn **L** into Pump Street. (Elgar's statue stands close to his father's piano shop, at the southern end of High Street.) Turn **L** again, into **The Shambles**. At junction turn **R** into Mealcheapen Street. Another **R**

turn and you are in **New Street** (which later becomes **Friar Street**).

**③** Head down this street (look out for King Charles' House where he stayed during the battle of Worcester in 1651). At end of street is dual carriageway (College Street). Turn **R** then cross carefully, to visit **cathedral**.

**④** Leave cathedral along College Precincts to fortified gateway known as **Edgar Tower**. (It is named after the 10th-century King Edgar, but was actually built in the 14th century. Go through this gateway to see College Green). Continue, along what is now **Severn Street**, which, unsurprisingly, leads to **River Severn**. Turn **R**, to complete your circuit, by following Kleve Walk, leafy waterside avenue; this section floods at some time most winters, and the **cricket ground** opposite was under several feet of water in 2000. For a more studied insight into the city's rich history, take a guided walk (on weekdays only) with a Green Badge Guide.

# 79 Kingsford Country Park and Villages

5½ miles (8.8km) 2hrs 30min **Ascent:** 410ft (125m) ▲

**Paths:** Forest rides, meadows, minor roads, village streets, canal tow path, 9 stiles

**Suggested map:** OS Explorer 218 Wyre Forest & Kidderminster or 219 Wolverhampton & Dudley

**Grid reference:** SO 835820 (on OS Explorer 218)

**Parking:** Blakeshall Lane car park, Kingsford Country Park

**A backwater that once knew busier times.**

**①** Take track inside northern edge of **country park** for 550yds (503m), to point about 50yds (46m) beyond end of extensive garden. To **L** is wide glade, falling gently; ahead rises woodland track.

**②** Turn **L** down ride. In 275yds (251m), at 5-way junction, go ahead (not along slight R fork). Join farm track. At road turn **R**, through **Blakeshall**. After 300yds (274m), at R-H bend near power lines, take stile into muddy and brick-strewn field. Keep hedge on your R, following yellow waymarkers into small valley. Reach, but don't go through, 7-bar metal gate before **Debdale Farm**. Turn sharply to **R**, uphill, following vague track. Enter **Gloucester Coppice** at gate and broken stile. Follow this track, soon more defined, all the way to southern end of Blakeshall Lane.

**③** Turn **L**, descending through street. The Holloway, into **Wolverley**. After village stores take 2nd footbridge on **R**. Reach Church of St John the Baptist

by zig-zagging up concreted footpath through deep cutting. Leave churchyard to **L** by steps. Go down meadow opposite (with fingerpost) to minor road.

**④** Turn **R** at B4189 turn **L** in front of **The Lock** pub turn **L**, along tow path. After about 1¼ miles (2km) is Debdale Lock, partly hewn into rock. Some 220yds (201m) further, just before steel wheel factory, is stile.

**⑤** Turn **L** along track. At T-junction after coniferous avenue turn **R** on broad gravel track. After about 440yds (402m) turn **L** (waymarker), up new wooden steps surfaced with scalpings, into trees. Go up **L-H** edge of one field and centre of another to road. Turn **L** for just 15yds (14m), then **R**. Some 400yds (366m) along this hedged lane take yellow option to **R** (to reduce road walking). At next stile wiggle **L** then **R**. Proceed ahead at junction to road. Turn **R**. In 150yds (137m), walk round wooden barrier to re-enter **country park**. Here, 2 paths run parallel to road – both lead back to car park.

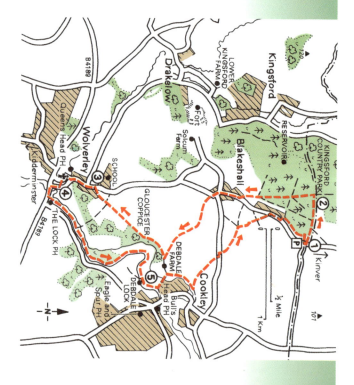

# Ombersley Along the River Severn

**5¾ miles (9.2km)** 2hrs 30min **Ascent:** 200ft (61m)

**Paths:** Riverside paths, field paths and tracks, village street, 9 stiles

**Suggested map:** OS Explorer 204 Worcester & Droitwich Spa

**Grid reference:** SO 845630

**Parking:** Towards southern end of road through Ombersley on eastern side (southbound exit from village)

## Explore an estate park.

**1** To south of village, and beyond cricket ground, take path on **R**. This is **Wychavon Way**. Briefly in trees, walk across meadow to stile beside willow. Go along **L-H** field edge, and briefly by water's edge. At corner of **fish pond** waymarker leads out to track. Turn **L**, following this track **R** in 80yds (73m). It becomes sunken path through delicious woodland. Cross meadow to river.

**2** Turn **R**. In 1 mile (1.6km) you'll pass 2 fishing pools to reach **Holt Fleet Bridge**. Go under this, continuing for another mile (1.6km), passing staffed **Holt Lock**. When opposite **Letchford Inn** you'll come to riverside stile.

**3** Don't go over it; instead, turn **R**. In field corner join access road. At junction keep ahead on public road. In 650yds (594m), at R-H bend, keep this line by moving **L**, on to farm track. The large area on the **R** was formerly an orchard, but it has gone completely.

It's over ¼ mile (400m) to top of this field. When you are 30yds (27m) before rusty shed, turn **R**. Now, in about 75yds (69m), go **L**, over stile.

**4** What could be a golf course fairway turns out to be an enormous garden. Aim to pass to **R** of house, by children's wooden watchtower. Cross gravel in front of house, **Greenfields**, to go down its private driveway. Turn **R** for 275yds (251m), passing several black-and-white houses, to T-junction – **Uphampton House** is in front of you.

**5** Turn **L** for 110yds (100m), then turn **R**, uphill. In 150yds (137m) don't bend **R** but go straight ahead, on shingly track. About 220yds (201m) further, main track bends **R**, rough track goes ahead and public footpath goes half **L**.

**6** Take public footpath option, along field edge. Continue through small area of market garden, reaching cul-de-sac. Shortly turn **R**, along village street to return to your car.

# Stourport-on-Severn Hartlebury Common

**Paths:** Tow path, tracks, good paths, some streets
**Suggested map:** OS Explorer 218 Wyre Forest & Kidderminster or 219 Wolverhampton & Dudley
**Grid reference:** SO 820704 (on Explorer 218)
**Parking:** Worcester Road car park on A4025 (poorly signed; height restriction bar spans narrow entrance)

**A Georgian 'new town' and a common.**

**1** Cross A4025. Turn **L** for 25yds (23m) to take footpath. Strike across bottom part of **Hartlebury Common**: you'll see buildings in far distance. Veer **R** through silver birches, to find sandy track at back of houses. At housing estate join tarmac briefly, aiming for dirt track beyond 2nd 'Britannia Gardens' sign and in front of Globe House. Shortly turn **L** down tarmac footpath, initially with wooden pailing on L, to **river**.

**2** Turn **R** in 650yds (594m) reach lock and Stourport's canal basins. Now, your route is neither across 2-plank walkway at upper lock gate, nor upper brick bridge with timber-and-metal railings; instead take neat brick-paved path to circumnavigate boarded-up. **Tontine** public house. Now skirt Upper Basin, passing Severn Valley Boat Centre. Across York Street join tow path. Follow this for just under ¾ mile (1.2km), leaving it at **Bird in Hand** pub, before defunct brick railway bridge.

**3** Go down Holly Road, then half **L** into Mill Road, going under railway then over **River Stour** to **B4193**. Cross and go to **L** of Myday Windows to take narrow, sandy, uphill path back on to common. Soon, at fork, go **L**, keeping direction as ground levels. Less than 50 paces after joining motor vehicle track reach trig point.

**4** Retrace your 50 paces and go another 30yds (27m), passing waymarker, to junction. Here turn **L**, away from car park. In just 40yds (37m) take **R** fork. In 100yds (91m) take **L** fork (not straight on). At corner of conifer plantation, 275yds further (251m), turn **R**. After 110yds (100m) turn **L**, then in 220yds (201m), turn **R**, just after far end of plantation, enjoy views. Now 65yds (60m) beyond this viewpoint take **R** option at subtle fork. Go forward for another 250yds (229m), until opening. Here step very carefully over pair of exposed and disused (and not actually hazardous) pipes. Follow sandy track slanting downhill for (110yds) 100m, then swing **R**, now head for car park.

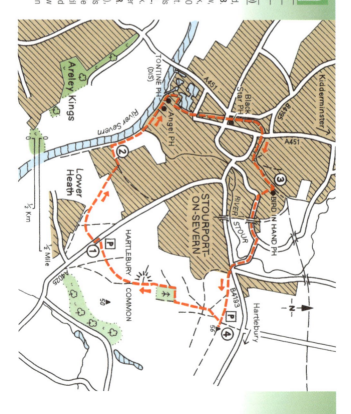

# Great Witley Among the Trees

**4¾ miles (7.7km)** 2hrs 45min **Ascent:** 1,150ft (350m)

**Paths:** Woodland paths, field paths, tracks, 9 stiles

**Suggested map:** OS Explorer 204 Worcester & Droitwich Spa

**Grid reference:** SO 752662

**Parking:** Car park of Hundred House Hotel (please phone beforehand, tel 01299 896888)

**Note:** Lots of wild geese on route so please keep dogs under control.

## A woodland walk up and down some hills.

**1** Cross A451 (take care). Through opening, strike sharply **R**, aiming for hedge end by last house. Step over fence; turn **L** on lane. Walk for ½ mile (800m) soon passing **Walsgrove Farm** and thousands of geese. Don't turn R up lane but go half **R**, taking path that becomes avenue of conifers, to top of **Woodbury Hill**. At marker post cross on to narrower track. In 130yds (119m) reach track above **Lippetts Farm**.

**2** Turn **R**, descending. At hairpin bend, aim away from farm to walk along inside edge of wood. Skirt to **L** of buildings at **Birch Berrow**, resuming on service road. As this goes up, R, to horse ring, take **R-H** of 2 gates. Go steeply down, taking stile into pines. Very soon, cross stile, turn **R** along road for 100yds (91m), so that you're past **1 Hillside Cottages**, not before it.

**3** Turn **R** again, back uphill. Continue north for nearly 1 mile (1.6km), over several stiles, walking

mostly in trees but later enjoying fine views westwards. Then, on top of **Walsgrove Hill**, you'll see the magnificent **clock tower** (1883) of **Abberley Hall**. Now go steeply down this meadow, to take stile into lane. Turn **R** for 80yds (73m) to B4203.

**4** Cross carefully. Turn **L**, along verge. Take driveway to **Abberley Hall School**. Leave driveway as it swings R, keeping this direction close to **clock tower** and all the way, on track, to A443. Take road opposite ('Wynniatts Way') up to brow of hill.

**5** Turn **R**. In about 400yds (366m) reach **trig point**. Walk along ridge path another 650yds (594m) to Worcestershire Way sign at path junction, just beyond which are 4 trees growing in a line across path.

**6** Take path down to R, initially quite steeply then contouring as it veers **R**, later descending again. Emerge from woods over stile to walk 2 large fields, meeting road beside **Hundred House Hotel**.

# Martley Through the Cider Orchards

**6¾ miles (10.9km)** 3hrs **Ascent:** 720ft (219m) ⚠

**Paths:** Field paths, lanes, orchard paths, tracks, river meadows, minor roads, 20 stiles

**Suggested map:** OS Explorer 204 Worcester & Droitwich Spa

**Grid reference:** SO 766597 **Parking:** St Peter's Church, Martley

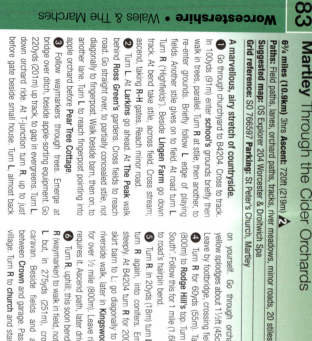

**A marvellous, airy stretch of countryside.**

**①** Go through churchyard to B4204. Cross to track. In 100yds (91m) enter **school's** grounds briefly then walk in trees, parallel. Turn **R** at stile, then another, to re-enter grounds. Briefly follow **L** edge of playing fields. Another stile gives on to field. At road turn **L**. Turn **R** ('Highfields'). Beside **Lingen Farm** go down track. At bend take stile, across field. Cross stream; ascend, taking **R-H** gates. Reach minor road.

**②** Turn **L**. At **Larkins** go ahead. At **The Peak** walk behind **Ross Green's** gardens. Cross fields to reach road. Go straight over, to partially concealed stile, not diagonally to fingerpost. Walk beside barn, then on, to another lane. Turn **L** to reach fingerpost pointing into apple orchard before **Pear Tree Cottage.**

**③** Follow waymarkers through trees. Emerge at bridge over ditch, beside apple-sorting equipment. Go 220yds (201m) up track, to gap in evergreens. Turn **L**, down orchard ride. At T-junction turn **R**, up to just before gate beside small house. Turn **L**, almost back

on yourself. Go through orchard, following faded yellow splodges about 1½ft (45cm) up on tree trunks. Leave by footbridge, crossing fields to B4197.

**④** Turn **R** for 60yds (55m). Take track for ½ mile (800m) to **Rodge Hill's** top. Turn sharp **L**, Worcs Way South. Follow this for 1 mile (1.6km). Steps lead down to road's hairpin bend.

**⑤** Turn **R** in 20yds (18m) turn **L**, but in 15yds (14m) turn **R** again, into conifers. Emerge to drop down steeply. At B4204 turn **R** for 200yds (183m). Turn **L**, riverside walk, later in **Kingswood Nature Reserve.** Follow skirt barn to **L**; go diagonally to **River Teme.** Follow for over ½ mile (800m). Leave river when wire fence requires it. Ascend path, later driveway, to road.

**⑥** Turn **R**, uphill; this soon bends **L**. Near brow move **R** (waymarker) to walk in field, not on road. At end turn **L** but, in 275yds (251m), cross 2 stiles beside caravan. Beside fields and allotments, emerge between **Crown** and garage. Pass telephone box into village. Turn **R** to **church** and start.

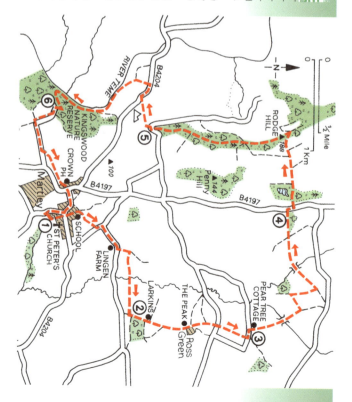

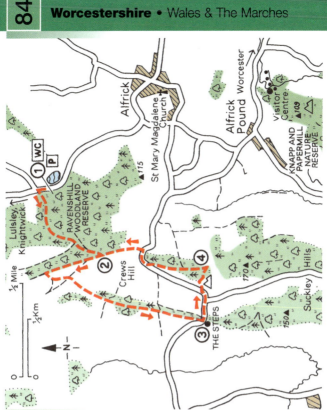

## Ravenshill A Wildlife Reserve

2¾ miles (4.4km) 1hr 30min **Ascent:** 475ft (145m) ▲

**Paths:** Firm or muddy tracks, meadows, some very short but steep, slippery sections, very little road, 8 stiles. Woodlands and rolling green fields

**Suggested map:** OS Explorer 204 Worcester & Droitwich Spa

**Grid reference:** SO 739539 **Parking:** Ravenshill Woodland Reserve (donation)

Elizabeth Barling's woodland dream.

**①** Walk towards **Luisley** for 150yds (137m). Turn **L** on green track beside Hill Orchard's private drive. Soon in woods, go 500yds (457m), joining another track beside wire enclosures. When stile and nearby gate lead into field on **R**, go 20yds (18m) further. Now go up to **L** on path (you may spot yellow band on branch). In 120yds (110m) climb rustic stile to turn partially **R**. Note well this point, where path joins obliquely from L, since you'll be returning this way – junction is easily missed! Go on for 100yds (91m) to driveway. Walk for 30yds (27m) away from house, to follow sign ('bridleway') down to **R**. Soon, at line of laurel bushes, reach tree-lined Worcestershire Way.

**②** Turn **R**. After 650yds (594m) go through gate. Peel **L**, hugging trees but not going under them. A narrow gap would lead into 2nd meadow but on R is fenced area. Climb waymarked stile beside padlocked gate. After another gate ascend diagonally **R**, veering

**L** as it levels. Maintain this line through metal gates across fields, then wooden gate into woodland. Eventually **The Steps** comes into view. Reach road by descending beside paddock fence, then through more gates, including red one.

**③** Turn **L**. Beyond Threshers Barn and Wain House is Crews Court. Beside fingerpost, go up steps to stile (Beware butting sheep). Go ahead, crossing private garden, to paddock. Go ahead but slightly **R**, to padlocked 7-bar gate; climb over this. Now move 20yds (18m) **R** to find your path up – proper stile, rendered obsolete by new fence. Go up quite steeply – you may need to scramble up last bit or find easier part. Now at ridge, don't fall off wobbly stile.

**④** Turn **L**. After 275yds (251m) fork down to **L**, not ahead. At road cross it before turning **R** to walk round bend. Turn **L** along driveway of The Crest then move **L** for Worcestershire Way again. Follow this to Point **②**. Retrace your steps to start.

# Tenbury Wells Berrington Court

**5¾ miles (9.2km)** 2hrs 30min **Ascent:** 280ft (85m) ▲

**Paths:** Town streets, field paths, minor lanes, 15 stiles

**Suggested map:** OS Explorer 203 Ludlow

**Grid reference:** SO 598682 **Parking:** Long-stay car park, beside swimming pool, Tenbury Wells

**A moderate stroll around a rural backwater.**

**1** Leave car park by 'no exit' sign. Over bridge turn **L**. At Crow Hotel turn **R** then **L**. Walk through **Tenbury Wells**. Cross beyond Pembroke House, soon taking 'Berrington'. Opposite bungalow, **'Somfield'**, cross stile. Go up and down to another, then walk on following power poles. Cross ditch over planks behind fallen trees. Go to field top.

**2** Turn **L** then **R**. Cross fields to join driveway of **Manor Farm**. 50yds (46m) beyond bridge turn **R** at triple waymarker to close stile. Cross fields for 440yds (402m). Veer down and **R**, through gap, then back up **L**, through **The Green's** several gates to lane.

**3** Go **L** for 750yds (686m). Just past '30mph' gates, head for far **L** field corner. Start up **L** edge. Over brow, at old tree line, strike diagonally to footbridge.

**4** Turn **R**, soon on Cadmore Lodge Hotel's **golf course**. Go straight and level, leaving course when just beyond hotel. Walk round **R** field edge, then down

farm track. Join minor road between imposing dwellings. Turn **L**. In 100yds (91m) take fingerpost, up steps. Cross field diagonally. Path leads to **Berrington Mill**. Turn **R**, up lane, then **R** to Frank P Matthews' nurseries at **Berrington Court**.

**5** Take track behind house. Enter **nursery**. Walk beside potted trees under glass. Leave gravel track where it cuts down through woodland. Meadows lead to **Bednal Bridge**. Just beyond it take double gates into trees. Keep your line when this ample track runs out. It's now straightforward to outskirts of **Tenbury**. (Yellow arrow pointing R eases sharp slope.) Round backs of gardens, emerge through gate.

**6** Turn **L** for 15yds (14m). Take kissing gate on **L**. Continue across flood plain, for 90yds (82m). Turn **R** (gate aperture is now behind you) to hit suburbia again. Turn **L**. Move **L** at 'No cycling'. Keep on tarmac footpath. **L** of No 14, soon beside garden fences. Emerging at **church**, turn **L**. Opposite church gate turn **R**, down Church Walk, to Teme Street.

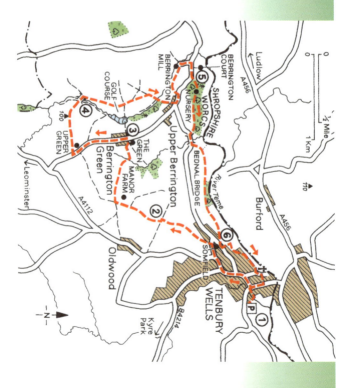

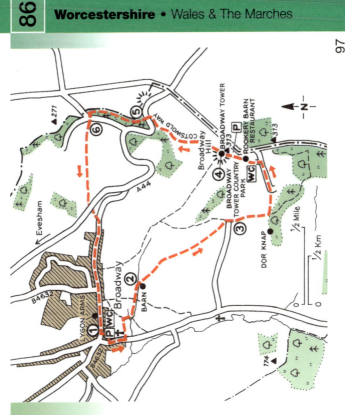

# Broadway William Morris

**5 miles (8km)** 2hrs 30min **Ascent:** 755ft (230m)

**Paths:** Pasture, rough, tree-root path, pavements, 8 stiles

**Suggested map:** OS Explorer OL45 The Cotswolds

**Grid reference:** SP 094374

**Parking:** Pay-and-display, short stay (4hrs max) in Church Close, Broadway; long stay options signposted

**A haunt of the Arts and Crafts pioneer.**

**①** Walk down Church Close. Turn **L**. At far end of wall turn **L**, soon passing orchard. At gate before grass turn **R**, to reach bridge over rivulet. Turn half **L**, across pasture. Go to **R-H** field corner. In 40yds (37m) reach bridge beside stone **barn**.

**②** Cross this to waymarker through boggy patch to 2 stiles. Continue to reach gate. Cross field. On joining vague, sunken lane bear **R**, to descend briefly to gate. Tree-lined track reaches 2nd gate within 60yds (55m).

**③** Slant uphill, passing in front of stone building. At woodland turn **L**. Join tarmac road, steadily uphill. At brow turn **L**, into **country park**. Pass **Rookery Barn Restaurant**. Take kissing gate into **Broadway Tower**.

**④** Beyond tower go through gate then take gate immediately on **R**. Move down, **L**, 20yds (18m) to walk in hollow, through pasture, to gate in dry-stone wall. Soon cross track and walk parallel to it in hollow, guided by **Cotswold Way** acorn waymarkers. Aim for

gates amongst trees. Beyond, keep ahead. In 45yds (41m), at next marker, bear **R**, walking above road. Soon cross it carefully, to footpath signs opposite.

**⑤** Leave **Cotswold Way** here. Care is needed in following these next instructions: descend, initially using steps. Ignore path on **L** after 50yds (46m). After another 50yds (46m) take yellow waymarker pointing up to **R**, over more steps. About 25 paces beyond steps use handrail to descend more steps. After 50yds (46m) you'll see orange Badger Trail disc. Proceed on this for 10yds (9m). Here orange disc points **L**, but follow yellow marker ahead. Follow path (beware of exposed tree roots) near top of wood. Eventually take steps on **L**, down to cross road junction.

**⑥** Take field path ('Broadway') through pastures. Swing **L** then **R** under new road. Emerge and turn **R**, on to dead end of Broadway's main street. In centre, 50yds (46m) beyond 3 red telephone boxes, turn **L**, through arcade, to Church Close car park.

# Wellington All Around The Wrekin

**8½ miles (13.7km)** **Ascent:** 1,585ft (485m) ▲

**Paths:** Woodland footpaths, urban streets, quiet lanes, 2 stiles

**Suggested map:** OS Explorer 242 Telford, Ironbridge & The Wrekin

**Grid reference:** SJ 651113

**Parking:** Belmont or Swimming Pool East car parks, both on Tan Bank, off Victoria Road, Wellington

**Note:** Rifle range on The Wrekin – warning notices posted, but take care on firing days

**A Shropshire classic.**

**❶** Walk along Tan Bank away from town centre. Cross Victoria Road and continue on Tan Bank then turn **L** on path just after **police station**. Walk to New Church Road; turn **R**. At **Holyhead Road**, turn **L**, then cross to **Limekiln Lane**. Don't miss **Old Hall School** (1480) on corner. Soon you see slopes of **The Wrekin** as **Limekiln Lane** heads under **M54** into countryside.

**❷** At end of lane, go ahead into **Limekiln Wood**; path leads along edge of wood at first. At junction, go to **L**, but few paces further fork **R** into wood. Ignore branching paths, sticking to well-trodden main route. At T-junction by ruined buildings, turn **R**, descend to junction and turn **L**, then **L** again at road.

**❸** Turn **R** on access road to **Wrekin Farm**. At **Wenlocks Wood**, leave road. Turn **R** on field-edge path heading towards **The Wrekin**. Cross stile on to its eastern slopes. Continue for a few paces then turn **L**.

**❹** Branch **R** where signpost indicates permissive path. Follow this round hill to cross path; turn **R** to join **Shropshire Way** over summit ridge. Approaching northern end, keep **L** when path forks, then **L** again by prominent beech tree, descending through woods. At edge of woods, leave **Shropshire Way**; turn **R** to lane.

**❺** Turn **R** to T-junction, join footpath opposite and go between 2 **reservoirs** before meeting lane; go **L**. When almost level with **Buckatree Lodge**, turn **R** into nature reserve. Go ahead along bridleway, past former **quarries** and pool. At junction, ignore path back towards quarries and continue for few paces to find that main track swings **L** and climbs to top of **Ercall**.

**❻** As Wellington comes into view, turn **R** on ridge-top path. As you descend, path forks. Go to **R** and join track under M54. Keep ahead along Golf Links Lane to **Holyhead Road**. Cross to footpath opposite. At road (Roseway) turn **R**, then **L** on to Tan Bank

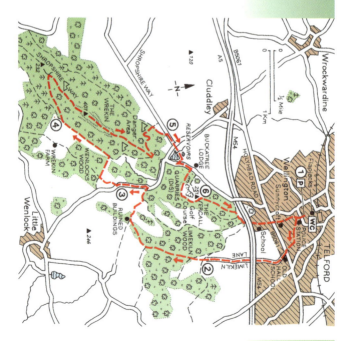

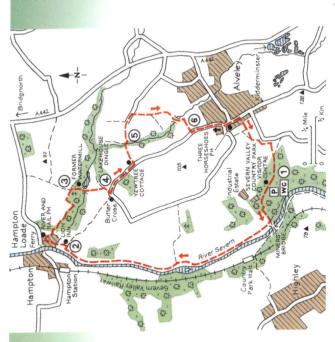

# Alveley Regeneration Route

**5 miles (8km)** 2hrs 30min **Ascent:** 425ft (130m) ▲

**Paths:** Riverside paths, green lanes, can be slippery in places and shallow streams in winter, 12 stiles

**Suggested map:** OS Explorer 218 Wyre Forest & Kidderminster

**Grid reference:** SO 753840

**Parking:** Visitor centre at Severn Valley Country Park, Alveley

## A great day out in the Severn Valley.

**1** Walk to river from **visitor centre**, using whichever route you prefer (History Trail), waymarked by red arrows, takes you directly to Miners' Bridge). Don't cross bridge, but descend steps to river bank and walk upstream for nearly 2 miles (3.2km).

**2** Follow short track to car park of **Lion Inn**. Turn **L** past Old Forge Cottage to **Hampton Loade**, then turn **R** past house called The Haywain (just before **River and Rail pub**). Waymarked path leads up through garden into wood, then along edge of field bordering wood. Go along two sides of field to reach top **L** corner, cross stile, turn **R** and cross another stile in next corner. Proceed to track and turn **R**.

**3** After few paces, look for waymarker indicating path on **R**. It descends through woodland to **Lakehouse Dingle**. Pass **former watermill**, cross footbridge and keep going along pebbly track. When you meet concrete track, turn **R** to junction with lane.

**4** Turn left, staying on lane until you've passed **Yewtree Cottage** and its neighbour. Take **L** turn after 2nd cottage. There is no signpost or waymarker here, but it's well-defined field-edge bridleway. At bottom of field look for gap in hedge, where way descends through trees to dingle.

**5** Turn **R**, climb up to meet lane and turn **R** again. After 100yds (91m), join track on **R**. When it bends **R**, keep straight on instead, along tree-lined green lane. Before long it becomes narrower and deeply rutted as it descends to brook. Cross at stepping stones, or at nearby footbridge. Track then swings **L** beside brook for while before turning sharp **R**.

**6** Turn **L** when you meet lane and walk into **Alveley**. Go through village centre, passing cottages, **church**, pub, shop and bus stop, then turning **R** on footpath next to premises of IGM. Path descends to junction where you turn **L** until you reach field through which well-trodden paths descend to **country park**.

# Wyre Forest The King's Wood

**5 miles (8km)** **Ascent:** 575ft (175m) ▲

**Paths:** Woodland and field paths, 2 stiles

**Suggested map:** OS Explorer 218 Wyre Forest & Kidderminster

**Grid reference:** SO 743784

**Parking:** Forestry Commission car park at Earnwood Copse, on south side of B4194, west of Buttonoak

## A leafy walk in Wyre Forest.

❶ Walk through gate on to forest road and immediately turn **R** on footpath (no signpost or waymarker) into **Earnwood Copse**. Keep straight on at all junctions, eventually joining sunken path not far from edge of forest. If you shortly pass under an overhanging yew tree you will know that you're on right path.

❷ Path descends to meet route of **Elan Valley pipeline**, bringing Welsh water to Birmingham. Turn **R** here and cross footbridge on edge of forest, to **R** of pipeline. Walk up bank into arable fields and then follow waymarked field-edge footpath uphill. At top, go through hedge gap and turn **L** towards **Kingswood**.

❸ Soon after passing timber-framed cottage (**Manor Holding**), come to T-junction at edge of forest. Go few paces to **L** towards **Kingswood Farm** and see track that swings **R** to enter forest. Keep straight on at all junctions, walking through **Brand Wood**.

❹ Soon reach **Dowles Brook**. Don't cross, turn **L** on bridleway that runs beside it. Follow bridleway for 1/4 miles (2km), with **Wimperhill Wood** on **L**.

❺ Turn **L** on another bridleway, which first passes through marshy area, then climbs through scrub and young woodland. It's waymarked and easily followed. After crossing forest road, go straight on, but turn **R** at next waymarked junction before swinging **L** to resume original heading. After crossing stream, bridleway turns **R** as it climbs above rim of steep valley.

❻ Turn sharp **L** (still on bridleway) through gap between 2 fenced areas. You are now approaching **Longdon Orchard** (conservation area, dogs must be under control). At next junction go **L**, into conifers, then soon turn **L**.

❼ Turn **R** when you meet Elan Valley pipeline again, then very soon **L**, still on bridleway. Follow it up to edge of forest near **Buttonoak**, then turn **L** to return to **Earnwood Copse**.

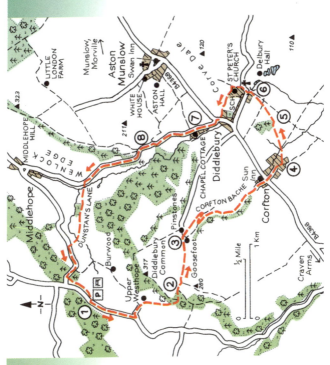

# Wenlock Edge Close to the Edge

**6¼ miles (10.1km)** 3hrs **Ascent:** 689ft (210m) ▲

**Paths:** Mostly good but ford on Dunstan's Lane can be deep after rain, 10 stiles

**Suggested map:** OS Explorer 217 The Long Mynd & Wenlock Edge

**Grid reference:** SO 479875

**Parking:** Car park/picnic site on east side of unclassified road between Middlehope and Westhope

### Along former drovers' roads to Corve Dale.

**1** Turn **L** out of car park along lane. At junction, turn **L** (**'Middlehope'**). Keep on at next (**'Upper Westhope'**) where road becomes track and bends **L** towards house. Go through gate on **R** instead and along grassy bridleway that enters woodland. Keep straight on at 2 cross paths.

**2** Bridleway emerges into pasture; keep straight on along **L-H** edge to corner. Go through gate and turn **R** on field-edge path, which soon becomes wide track.

**3** Pass cottage and barns ahead, look for blue arrows directing sharp **R**. Keep **L** above **Corfton Bache**, deep valley, until blue arrows send you down into valley. Follow it to road at **Corfton** and cross to lane opposite.

**4** As lane degenerates into track, look on **L** for footpath starting at kissing gate. Go diagonally **L** across pasture to prominent stile at far side. Cross farm track and walk to far **R** corner of arable field.

**5** Go through gate, then little way along **L-H** edge of another field until gate gives access to parkland. Follow waymarker. **St Peter's Church** at **Diddlebury** comes into view, providing guide.

**6** Cross 2 stiles at far side of park; descend slope, to **R** of fence. Cross bridge to **Diddlebury**. Turn **R**, then **L** by church. Join footpath: pass to **R** of village hall, then diagonally **R** past **school**, over 2 stiles and across fields to road. Cross to lane; fork **R** after few paces.

**7** Footpath leaves lane on **R**, almost opposite **Chapel Cottage**. Turn **R** to visit **Swan Inn** or continue.

**8** At junction with bridle track by sign ('Aston Top') keep **L** on lane. After ¾ mile (1.2km), branch **L** on byway, **Dunstan's Lane** (no signpost or waymarker). Follow it to Middlehope road; turn **L**. Keep on at Y-junction. When footpath crosses road, turn **L** into woodland. Path is signposted on **R**, but not **L** – **L** branch is few paces further on. Go through woods back to picnic site.

# Ellesmere Meres, Mosses and Moraines

**7¼ miles (11.7km)** 3hrs **Ascent:** 180ft (55m) ▲

**Paths:** Field paths and canal tow path, 8 stiles

**Suggested map:** OS Explorer 241 Shrewsbury

**Grid reference:** SJ 407344

**Parking:** Castlefields car park opposite The Mere

## A wonderful watery walk.

**①** Cross to **The Mere;** turn **L.** Pass **The Boathouse** and **visitor centre** and walk towards town, until you reach Cremorne Gardens. Join path that runs through trees close by water's edge for ¾ mile (1.2km).

**②** Leave trees for field and turn **L,** signposted '**Welshampton'.** Path soon joins track to **Crimps Farm.** Turn **R** past farm buildings to cross stile on **R** of track. Continue along another track.

**③** Track leads into sheep pasture where you go straight on, guided by waymarkers and stiles. When you come to field with trig pillar, waymarker is slightly misleading – ignore it and go straight across. In next field aim for 3 prominent trees close together at far side. As you approach them, turn **L** into field corner.

**④** Go through gate and descend by **R-H** hedge. When it turns corner, go with it, to **R.** Skirt **pool** and keep going in same direction on grassy track, passing another pool. Track soon becomes much better

defined and leads to farm where you join road.

**⑤** Turn **L** and keep ahead at junction into **Welshampton.** Turn **R** on **Lyneal Lane** and follow it to bridge over **Llangollen Canal.** Descend steps to tow path. Turn **R,** passing under bridge. Pass **Lyneal Wharf, Cole Mere, Yell Wood** and **Blake Mere,** then through **Ellesmere Tunnel.** Beyond this are 3 footpaths signposted 'The Mere'. Take any of these short cuts, but to see bit more of canal, including visitor moorings and **marina,** stay on tow path.

**⑥** Arriving at **bridge 58,** further choices present themselves. You could extend this walk to include signposted Wharf Circular Walk or to explore town: just follow signs. To return directly to The Mere, however, go up to road and turn **L.**

**⑦** Fork **R** on road by **Blackwater Cottage.** Turn **R** at top, then soon **L** at Rose Bank, up steps. Walk across earthworks of long-gone **Ellesmere Castle** and follow signs for The Mere or car park.

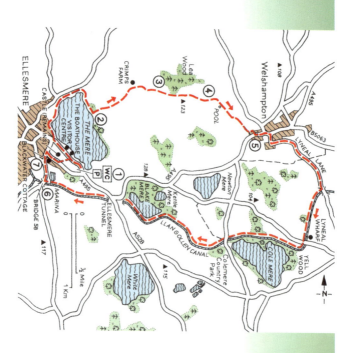

# Whittington From Castle to Canal

**6 miles (9.7km)** 2hrs 30min **Ascent:** Negligible

**Paths:** Tow path, lanes and field paths, very overgrown, 19 stiles

**Suggested map:** OS Explorer 240 Oswestry

**Grid reference:** SJ 325312

**Parking:** Car park next to Whittington Castle – honesty box

**Follow the Llangollen branch of the Shroppie through pastoral countryside.**

**1** Turn **R** by Shrewsbury road (B5009), using footway on left. After about ½ mile (800m), cross stile and follow waymarked path across 3 fields to far **R** corner of 3rd field.

**2** Walk along edge of next field, with wood on your **L**. Cross stile in corner, then go obliquely across another field as indicated by waymarker. prominent oak tree is useful guide. There is stile near tree, but you may have to wade through nettles to get to it. Continue in same direction across next field to lane and turn **L**.

**3** Keep **L** when you come to fork and continue to A495. Turn **R** for few paces, then cross to other side. Join footpath that runs along **L-H** edge of field to stile and footbridge. Beyond these, keep going along field edge until gap in hedge. Go through, but continue in same direction as before, soon going up bank.

**4** Meet canal at **Pollett's Bridge** (No 6). Don't cross it – go under to join tow path. Follow this to **Hindford Bridge** (No 11), then go up to lane. Turn **R** past **Jack Myton Inn**, then **R** again, signposted 'Iron Mills and Gobowen'.

**5** Take footpath on left. Walk down long, narrow paddock to far end, then cross stile on right. Follow fence to footbridge, then continue across next pasture to another footbridge and keep straight on to stile ahead. Go up to far **R** corner of next field, through gate and then **L** by field edge.

**6** Join track that soon bends **R** beside course of **dismantled railway**. Look out for stile giving access to railway. Turn **R** on former trackbed for few paces, then up bank on **L** – watch out for steps concealed in undergrowth here. Cross stile to field, turn **R** to far side and cross another stile. Bear **L** to large oak tree, then continue to lane. Follow it to Top Street and turn right, then **L** to **Whittington Castle**.

# Stiperstones Back to Purple

**4½ miles (7.2km)** 2hrs **Ascent:** 951ft (290m) ▲

**Paths:** Good paths across pasture, moorland and woodland, 1 stile
**Suggested map:** OS Explorer 216 Welshpool & Montgomery
**Grid reference:** SJ 373022
**Parking:** Car park at Snailbeach

**From the mining village of Snailbeach to the dragon's crest of Stiperstones.**

❶ Take Lordshill lane opposite car park, then join parallel footpath on L. Rejoining lane, cross to site of locomotive shed, then continue up lane, noticing green arrows directing you to main sites.

❷ Turn **R** on track between **crusher house** and **compressor house.** Few paces past compressor house, turn **L** up steps. At top, turn **R**, then soon **L** up more steps. Turn **L** to Cornish engine house, then **R** and continue through woodland. Short detour leads to smelter **chimney**, otherwise it's uphill all way.

❸ Sign indicates that you're entering **Stiperstones National Nature Reserve** (NNR). Woods give way to bracken, broom and bramble before you cross over stile on to open hill. Path climbs slope ahead to stile/gate at top.

❹ Two paths are waymarked. Take **L-H** one, which runs between fence and rim of spectacular dingle on

your **R**. Path then climbs away from dingle and meets rutted track. Turn **R.** As path climbs you can see rock tors on summit. There's also one much closer to hand, isolated from rest. This is **Shepherd's Rock.**

❺ Just beyond **Shepherd's Rock** is junction marked by cairn. Turn **R** here, then fork **L** to go round other side of rock. Leave NNR at gate/stile. The path runs to **L,** shortly bordered by hawthorn hedge. You'll soon see that this is an old green lane, lined at various points by either hedges/trees on both sides, one line of trees or tumbledown stone wall.

❻ At junction take **L-H** path back into NNR. At next junction, fork **R** to leave NNR at gate by plantation. Go diagonally across field to track; turn **R,** going back across field, through plantation, then across pasture on bridleway.

❼ Fork **L** at bridleway junction and continue past **Lordshill chapel** to lane. Turn **R** and stay with it as it swings **L** to **Snailbeach.**

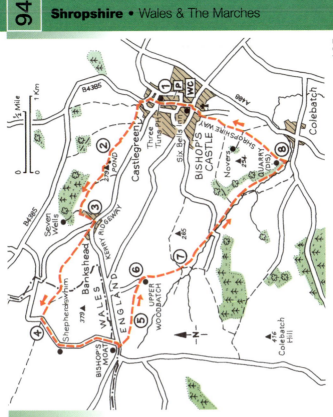

# Bishop's Castle Life and Death

**7 miles (11.3km)** 2hrs 30min **Ascent:** 738ft (225m) ⛰

**Paths:** Waymarking can be patchy, path near Woodbatch cropped over, gates to climb, about 10 stiles

**Suggested map:** OS Explorer 216 Welshpool & Montgomery

**Grid reference:** SO 324886

**Parking:** Car park off Station Street

**A colourful border town.**

**❶** Walk up Church Street, High Street and Bull Street, go **L** on Bull Lane to **Castlegreen**. Turn **R**, then **L** after No 11 on footpath to reach stile. Take **L-H** path, cross 2 fields, go ahead along green lane. At end, go through gate and along field edge to stile.

**❷** Turn **R** in next field, cross stile at top and go obliquely **L** over field to fence corner. Follow fence/hedge past **pond** to stile. Go obliquely **L** across highest point of next field, then down to gate halfway along far hedge. Go diagonally **R** across another field to hedge, next to crab apple trees. Follow hedge to track and turn **L** to road.

**❸** Turn **R**, immediately **R** again and **L** on to lane, which soon becomes track. Descend into woodland, cross into Wales and eventually meet lane.

**❹** Turn **L** and walk up to meet road, **Kerry Ridgeway**, at **Bishop's Moat**, where you cross back into England. Turn **R**, then through 1st gate on **L** (it

hangs from one hinge). Go diagonally **L** to end of line of hawthorn trees, continue in same direction over another field to kink in far hedge.

**❺** Go diagonally across 3rd field to line of trees which leads to gate. Continue down next field to far **R** corner, walking through scrap-metal collection.

**❻** Meeting farm lane, turn **R** through farmyard at **Upper Woodbatch**, passing barns. Approaching final group, see track descending by fence. Right of way is on other side of fence, so go through gate to join it and follow it down through 2 fields towards brook.

**❼** About 120yds (110m) before brook, turn **L** across field. Go through gate and continue across 2 fields to lane. Join **Shropshire Way** opposite, following it along bottom of several fields, quite close to brook.

**❽** Pass abandoned **quarry**, turn **L** uphill and head for **Bishop's Castle**, soon joining track leading to Field Lane. Follow this to Church Lane, which leads to Church Street and start.

# The Long Mynd An Ancient Settlement

7½ miles (12.1km) 3hrs **Ascent:** 1,545ft (471m) ▲3

**Paths:** Mostly moorland paths and tracks, 3 stiles

**Suggested map:** OS Explorer 217 The Long Mynd & Wenlock Edge

**Grid reference:** SO 453936

**Parking:** Easthope Road car park, Church Stretton

**Prehistoric remains and magnificent views.**

❶ Walk up Lion Meadow to High Street and turn **R**. Turn **L** at The Square, go past church and straight on into **Rectory Field**. Walk to top **L** corner, turn **R** by edge, soon entering **Old Rectory Wood**. Path descends to junction. Turn **L**, soon crossing Town Brook, then climb again to gate on to **Long Mynd**.

❷ Go forward beside brook to railings, continue with brook **L**. After slight height gain, path begins to climb more steeply and heads away from brook. Eventually path and brook meet up again near head of latter.

❸ Path crosses brook. Go 50yds (46m) to junction marked by 1st in succession of pink-banded posts. Follow these posts, gaining height gradually again. Ignore branching paths and, after slight rise, you'll see summit ahead on **L**.

❹ Meet unfenced road about 100yds (91m) **L** of junction. Turn **L**, ignore path to Little Stretton and go straight on when road bends **L**, joining bridleway. At

next junction, turn **L** to summit, then keep straight on to **Port Way**. Turn **R** past site of Pole Cottage.

❺ Turn **L** on footpath, signposted to **Little Stretton**. When wide rutted track forks go **L** – you can see path ahead, cutting grassy green swath over shoulder of **Round Hill**. Go straight on at junction, then descend to **Cross Dyke** (Bronze-Age earthwork). After dyke, path ascends briefly but soon levels out, then descends, eventually following brook to Little Stretton.

❻ Cross at footbridge by ford and turn **R** on lane for few paces. Look for footpath on **L**. It climbs by field edge to top corner, then turns **L**, following top of steep slope to pasture. Follow **R-H** edge of this until path enters woodland. Descend to **Ludlow Road**.

❼ Here join bridleway next to footpath. It climbs into woodland, emerging at far side to meet track, which becomes road. As it bends **R** there's access **L** to **Rectory Field**. Descend to The Square, turn **R** on High Street and **L** on Lion Meadow to car park.

# The Strettons The Shapeliest Hills

**6 miles** (9.7km) **3hrs Ascent:** 1,060ft (323m) ⚠️ **2**

**Paths:** Good paths through pasture and woodland, lane, 14 stiles

**Suggested map:** OS Explorer 217 The Long Mynd & Wenlock Edge

**Grid reference:** SO 453936

**Parking:** Easthope Road car park, Church Stretton

**If you like proper pointy hills, the exciting Strettons will make your day.**

❶ Walk along Easthope Road to Sandford Avenue, turn **R** past station. Cross A49, go along Sandford Avenue, turn **R** on Watling Street South. Turn **L** by post-box, fork **R** on Clive Avenue, and **L** on Ragleth Road.

❷ Turn **R** into Woodland Trust reserve, Philla's Grove. Keep **L** at fork, climbing by edge of wood, and **L** at next junction. Leave wood at stile and turn **R** on footpath. After level section, path climbs steeply to stile. Turn **R** for few paces, then fork **L** to higher path, which goes by L-H fence through woodland.

❸ When path emerges on hillside, keep ahead to stile, but don't cross it. Turn your back on it and follow path up **Ragleth Hill**, then walk along spine of hill.

❹ Pole marks southern summit (smaller of 2), but descent isn't obvious. Go **L**, across rocky area to far fence, then follow it down to corner where stile leads into field. Turn **L** across field corner, cross stile and

climb to top **L** corner of next field. Go ahead to far **L** corner of field to lane.

❺ Turn **L** on to lane and continue ahead, ignoring R turns.

❻ Take 2nd path branching off **L** and walk through gorse and bracken to gate. Path continues through woodland.

❼ Approaching 2nd gate, don't go through, but turn **R** round **Hazler Hill**. Turn **R** at lane, walk to junction and cross to bridleway opposite, which passes **Gaerstones Farm**. After **Caer Caradoc** comes into view, look for bridleway, **L**, to gate/stile 40yds (37m) away. Descend past **Helmeth Hill** to another bridleway at point where this is crossed by brook.

❽ Turn **L**, emerge from woodland into pasture. Continue with fence **L**. Path leads to lane, turn **L** to **Church Stretton**. Turn **R** at Sandford Avenue, cross road, pass station then **L** on Easthope Road to start.

# Stokesay Over the Edge

6¼ miles (10.1km) 2hrs 30min **Ascent:** 909ft (277m) ▲

**Paths:** Mostly excellent, short stretch eroded and uneven, byway from Aldon to Stoke Wood occasionally floods, 12 stiles

**Suggested map:** OS Explorers 203 Ludlow; 217 The Long Mynd & Wenlock Edge

**Grid reference:** SO 437819 (on Explorer 217) **Parking:** Lay-by on A49 north of Stokesay turn

A 13th-century house set in gorgeous hills.

**①** Take footway from lay-by to lane that leads to **Stokesay Castle**. Walk past castle; take 2nd footpath on R, at far side of **pool**. It skirts farm, then crosses railway. Keep ahead through 3 meadows on worn path, with series of stiles providing further guidance.

**②** Enter **Stoke Wood**, proceed to track; turn **R**. Leave wood at stile at far end and walk past house. Turn **R** at top, walking by edge of **View Wood**.

**③** Join track that leads into wood, then emerges from it to run alongside edge. It soon plunges back into trees, climbing quite steeply, then levelling out to reach lane by **Viewedge Farm**.

**④** Turn **L** for few paces, then join footpath on **R**. Turn **R** by field edge and walk to top of knoll, continuing in same direction across fields to waymarker that sends you sharp **L** across adjacent field. Join track at far side and continue past **Gorst Barn** to lane. Turn **R**.

**⑤** Turn **L** on footpath, crossing 3 pastures to concealed stile, which gives on to bridleway. Turn **L** down **Brandhill Gutter**. Eventually go through gate on **R**, but immediately turn **L** to continue in same direction. Keep close to stream (or, very often, dry streambed) on **L**.

**⑥** After passing through gate, bridleway becomes narrow, uneven and eroded for while but soon improves. It eventually crosses stream (next to stile) and starts to swing northwards, into **Aldon Gutter**. Beyond **abandoned cottage**, bridleway passes to R of pheasant pens – watch carefully for waymarkers here.

**⑦** 200yds (183m) after cottage, bridleway bears **R**, climbing steep valley side to meet lane at top. Turn **R** to pass through hamlet of **Aldon**, then **L** at T-junction.

**⑧** Join byway on **R** at slight bend in lane (no sign or waymarker). This lovely hedged track leads between fields, then through **Stoke Wood**, beyond which it descends to **Stokesay** and start.

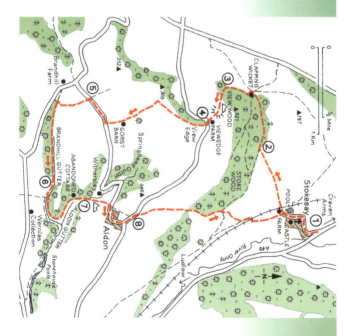

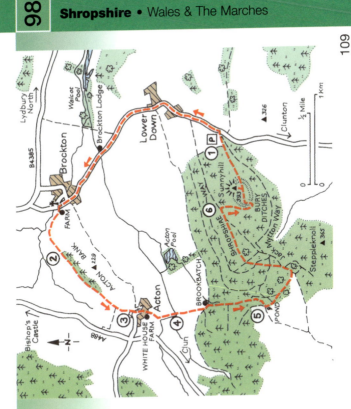

## Sunnyhill To Bury Ditches

**5½ miles (8.8km)** 2hrs **Ascent:** 804ft (245m) ⚠️

**Paths:** Field and woodland paths, one boggy and overgrown, fence and gates to climb; 8 stiles

**Suggested map:** OS Explorer 216 Welshpool & Montgomery

**Grid reference:** SO 334839

**Parking:** Forestry Commission car park at Sunnyhill off minor road north from Clunton

### Magnificent views from a dramatic hill fort.

**1** From car park, walk back to lane; turn **L**. Descend through hamlet of **Lower Down** and continue to **Brockton**. Turn **L** on track shortly before you come to ford. Pass collection of semi-derelict buses behind **farm**, then go through gate on **L** and walk along **R-H** edges of three fields, parallel with track.

**2** Climb over fence into wood and continue in same direction, contouring round base of **Acton Bank**. After leaving wood path continues through scrub, then through pasture below some old quarries, before it meets lane at hamlet of **Acton**.

**3** Turn **L**, pass to **R** of triangular green and join path running past **White House Farm**. Frequent waymarkers guide you past house, across field, then **L** over stile and along **R-H** edge of another field.

**4** Cross footbridge and continue straight across ensuing field towards building at far side. Cross stile in hedge, turn **L** for few paces and then **R** on track

which passes by house called **Brookbatch** and rises into woodland. When track eventually bends to **L**, go forward over stile instead and continue climbing.

**5** Emerging on to track, turn **L** past **pond**. Cross cattle grid into Forestry Commission property and leave track, turning **R** on footpath leading through beechwoods. It winds through trees to meet **Shropshire Way** (waymarked with buzzard logo). Turn **L**, then soon **R** at junction. Ignoring **R** turn, stay on Shropshire Way, which soon forks **L** off main track.

**6** You now have choice of 2 buzzards to follow: main route of Shropshire Way goes straight on, but you should choose alternative route which branches **R**. Path leads to **Bury Ditches** hill fort, then cuts through gap in ramparts and crosses interior. At colour-banded post (red, blue and green), path branches **L** to allow visit to summit, with its toposcope and incredible views. Bear **R** to return to main path and turn **L** to follow it to car park.

# Offa's Dyke Walking with Offa

**8 miles (12.9km)** 3hrs **Ascent:** 1,542ft (470m) ▲

**Paths:** Excellent, mostly across short turf, 8 stiles

**Suggested map:** OS Explorer 201 Knighton & Presteigne

**Grid reference:** SO 287734

**Parking:** Informal parking in Kinsley Wood, accessed by forest road from A488 (or park in Knighton, next to bus station or near Offa's Dyke Centre)

### Offa's Dyke on the Welsh border.

**❶** Adjacent to car park, at northern end of **Kinsley Wood**, is meadow with barn. Join bridleway which runs along **L-H** edge of this meadow. After 200yds (183m), veer slightly away from field edge and descend through trees to **Offa's Dyke Path** (ODP).

**❷** Turn **R**: follow ODP for 2½ miles (4km). Path runs just above steep slope falling away to west and just below top of **Panpunton Hill**, and follows dyke all way. After climbing around head of combe, it gains top of **Cwm-sanaham** Hill (1,328ft/406m), then continues northwards, soon descending past house, **Brynorgan**.

**❸** Meeting road, leave ODP, turning **L**, then **L** again at **Selley Cross**. After ½ mile (800m), just beyond **Selley Hall Cottage**, join footpath on **R**. Follow path to far side of field, then turn **R**, heading to top **R** corner. Cross stile, then continue straight across several fields, to meet lane at **Monaughty Poeth**.

**❹** Turn **L** for ¾ mile (1.2km) to junction at **Skyborry Green**. Turn **L**, then immediately **R**, joining bridleway to **Bryney farm**. Turn **R** on footpath (waymarked at regular intervals as it contours round hill), before descending to road again at **Nether Skyborry**.

**❺** Turn **L** for ½ mile (800m), then **R** on to ODP just before **Panpwnton farm**. Cross railway and River Teme, then follow Teme towards **Knighton**. Still on path cross border and turn **R** to **Offa's Dyke Centre**.

**❻** Leaving **centre**, turn **L** through Knighton, then **L** again on Station Road. After passing **station**, turn **L** on Kinsley Road. Join 1st path on **R** into **Kinsley Wood**, opposite Kinsley Villa and Gillow. Fork **L** after few paces, then embark on almost vertical climb. Gradient eases before path emerges from trees to continue through scrub and across forest road. Keep ahead to top of ridge; turn **L** to walk across summit. Path descends to track. Turn **R** to return to parking area.

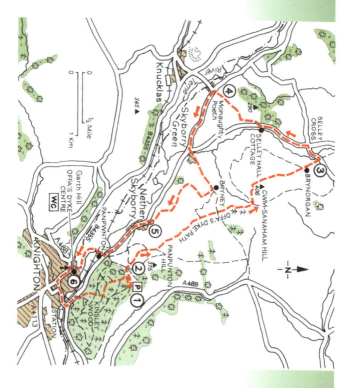

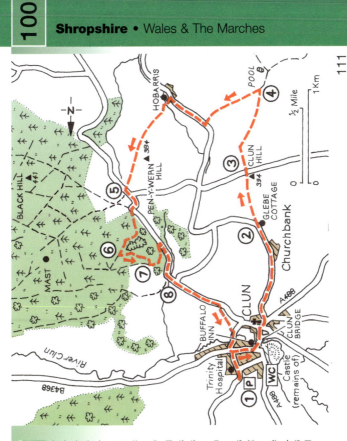

# Clun Under the Sun

**5½ miles (8.8km)** 2hrs 30min **Ascent:** 1,066ft (325m) ▲

**Paths:** Excellent, through mixed farmland (mainly pasture) and woodland, 3 stiles

**Suggested map:** OS Explorer 201 Knighton & Presteigne

**Grid reference:** SO 302811

**Parking:** Car park at Clun community area, signed from High Street

**From the tranquil Clun Valley into the hills.**

❶ Walk down Hospital Lane to High Street and turn **R** to The Square. Pass **Buffalo Inn**, turn **L** on Buffalo Lane and cross **Clun Bridge**. Go up Church Street, turn **R** on Knighton road, then turn **L** on Hand Causeway, signposted to **Churchbank** and **Hobarris**.

❷ After ¾ mile (1.2km), take bridleway on **R**, which leaves lane on bend by **Glebe Cottage** and immediately goes **L** into field. Walk up field, through gate at top, then on through 2 more fields to lane running across top of **Clun Hill** (part of prehistoric Clun–Clee Ridgeway).

❸ Path continues opposite, along **R-H** edges of 2 fields. At end of 2nd, go through gate on **R** and diagonally to far corner of another field, then in same direction down next – towards pool in valley below.

❹ Go through gate; turn **L** on byway, then **R** at T-junction. At **Hobarris** go **L** on to track, just before main farm buildings. Soon after crossing brook, branch **L**

along hollow way. When this bends R, go straight on, over stile into field. Go straight uphill, joining field-edge track. To your L, 3 Scots pines and prehistoric cairn mark summit of **Pen-y-wern Hill**. Turn **L** at lane.

❺ At crossroads, keep ahead, descending by 2nd of 2 bends in lane. Ignore signposted path on R; instead take unsignposted path few paces further on. It leads into plantation and soon bends **R**. About 200yds (183m) after this, branch **L** on descending path.

❻ After 200yds (183m) branch **L**, down through oakwood. Continue to meet path at bottom of wood.

❼ Turn **L** on path, which almost immediately swings **L**, back into wood and winds through trees to meet lane. Turn **R** towards **Clun**.

❽ Turn **L** at junction with 2 tracks. Keep along lane until stile on **R** gives access to field. Go diagonally **L** towards Clun. Join lane, then turn **R** and cross footbridge by ford. Turn **R** to High Street and Hospital Lane.

# Walking in Safety

All these walks are suitable for any reasonably fit person, but less experienced walkers should try the easier walks first. Route finding is usually straightforward, but you will find that an Ordance Survey map is a useful addition to the route maps and descriptions.

## Risks

Although each walk has been researched with a view to minimising the risks to the walkers who follow its route, no walk in the countryside can be considered to be completely free from risk. Walking in the outdoors will always require a degree of common sense and judgement to ensure that it is as safe as possible.

- Some sections of route are by, or cross roads. Take care and remember traffic is a danger even on minor country lanes.

- Be careful around farmyard machinery and livestock; especially if you have children or a dog with you.

- Be particularly careful on cliff paths and in upland terrain, where the consequences of a slip can be very serious.

- Be aware of the consequences of changes of weather and check the forecast before you set off. Carry spare clothing and a torch if you are walking in the winter months. Remember that the weather can change very quickly at any time of the year,

- Remember to check tidal conditions before walking along

the seashore.

and in moorland and heathland areas, mist and fog can make route finding much harder. Don't set out in these conditions unless you are confident of your navigation skills in poor visibility. In summer remember to take account of the heat and sun; wear a hat and carry spare water.

- On walks away from centres of population you should carry a whistle and survival bag. If you do have an accident requiring the emergency services, make a note of your position as accurately as possible and dial 999.